The Joy of Cranberries

The Tangy Red Treat

by Theresa Millang

Adventure Publications, Inc.
Cambridge, Minnesota

A special thank you to all.

In this salute to cranberries I have included my own recipes as well as those gathered from across the country. My thanks to all for sharing your favorites for this collection.

Book and Cover Design by Jonathan Norberg

Copyright 2004 by Theresa Nell Millang
Published by Adventure Publications, Inc.
820 Cleveland Street South
Cambridge, Minnesota 55008

1-800-678-7006
ISBN: 1-59193-055-3
Printed in the United States of America

Table of Contents

PIES

DESSERTS

5

TARTS, TORTES
Tarts

Tortes

MUFFINS, BREADS, SCONES, BISCUITS
Muffins

STUFFING, SIDES

Stuffing

Sides

BEVERAGES

SAUCES, CONDIMENTS
Sauces

Salsa

Chutney

Introduction

Cranberries ripen when the nights are turning crisp with a definite scent of autumn in the air. This fruit, native to North America, has long enjoyed a prominent place at holiday meals. More recently, though, the health benefits of cranberries have been widely discovered, and American families have consumed between 400 and 600 million pounds of the bright red berries each year. Many regions and growers host harvest celebrations and festivals. Surely there is something special about this red fruit.

About Cranberries

Cranberries have a long history as an important food for people. Early in the cranberry's history, various Native American groups utilized the bright red fruit. The juice made an excellent dye for fabrics; the berry had medicinal values; and the fruits were eaten in a variety of ways. Pemmican, an important food staple, was made from mashed berries mixed and dried with meat, fat and grains.

Settlers quickly grasped the value of this berry. It was named craneberry for the blossom's resemblance to a crane's head, but the name cranberry was being used by about 1650. In 1816, cranberries were first cultivated by Captain Henry Hall of Massachusetts, and by the 1820s, cranberries were being shipped to Europe for sale. Before the cranberry was widely cultivated, strict regulations for the harvest—and fines for breaking the rules—were put in place to protect the cranberry bogs from overharvest.

Cranberries grow on woody vines in sandy bogs or marshes; they do not grow in water. They thrive in cooler northern climates and need acid peat soil, sand and a good supply of fresh water. Blossoms and subsequent berries are produced on upright shoots that are two to eight inches tall. It takes three to five years for a cranberry vine to bear a full crop. The vines are long-lived; some in Cape Cod are more than 150 years old. While there are many fruits native to North America, only cranberries, blueberries and blue Concord grapes are commercially harvested on a large scale.

Wisconsin and Massachusetts harvest the most cranberries in the U.S. Harvest begins in September and continues into October or November. White cranberries are harvested the earliest; they are actually "regular" cranberries that have ripened but have not yet turned red. Cranberries were first picked by hand, then with toothed wooden scoops that combed the fruit from the vine. Today they are mainly harvested in two ways. Berries that are destined to be sold fresh are dry harvested by mechanical pickers with comb-shaped attachments that gather the fruit.

Cranberries that are made into juices, jellies and the like are wet harvested, a process that was first successful in the 1960s. This is the faster of the two methods. The growers flood the cranberry bogs with a foot or more of water when the fruit is ripe. Harvesting machines with large reels stir up the water with enough force to loosen the berries, which then float to the surface where they are gathered for transport. During the winter, cranberry growers flood the bogs and wait for the top eight inches or so to freeze. The water underneath is then drained, which allows the vines to breathe while they are still protected from freezing and drying winter air.

Cranberry bogs, aside from producing the popular red berries, can be very important habitat areas. Each acre of cultivated cranberry bog is supported by four or more acres of surrounding land. Since the support land is used for little else, these areas provide important habitat pockets for a number of rare or endangered plants, insects, birds and other animals. Many cranberry growers use sustainable and environmentally responsible methods for pest control and fertilization to protect the health of their own bogs and the surrounding land.

The Healthful Benefits of Cranberries

Cranberries are a good source of calcium, potassium and vitamin C. According to the USDA's National Nutrient Database for Standard Reference, one cup of unsweetened cranberry juice contains 20 mg of calcium, 195 mg of potassium and 23.5 mg of vitamin C. A cup of canned, sweetened cranberry sauce contains 11 mg of calcium, 72 mg of potassium and 5.5 mg of vitamin C.

Most people know about the cranberry's ability to ward off and treat urinary tract infections (UTIs). Cranberries contain structurally unique compounds called proanthocyanidins. These compounds prevent the bacteria that cause UTI from adhering to urinary tract cells, so the bacteria can't reproduce and lead to infection. These same compounds also inhibit the adhesion of certain bacteria that cause peptic ulcers and dental plaque. The cranberry's anti-adhesion properties may produce exciting and important advances in the ways we battle infections.

Cranberries are also among the fruits and vegetables that are high in antioxidants. Antioxidants stabilize free radicals, which are thought to cause or accelerate many health problems, mostly associated with aging. Our bodies produce free radicals through normal metabolic processes, but we also accumulate free radicals from our environment. Toxic levels of free radicals have been blamed for cell damage that causes cancer, heart disease and age-related disorders. Cranberries, which are loaded with antioxidants, can help protect our bodies from damage caused by harmful levels of free radicals. In addition, the antioxidants found in cranberries may reduce the risk of atherosclerosis—the accumulation of "bad cholesterol" (LDL) in arteries.

Whichever way you enjoy eating cranberries, you'll reap the benefits of this tangy red fruit. Enjoy and spread the word!

Sources: The Cranberry Institute, www.cranberryinstitute.org/healthresearch.htm (Accessed 28 April, 2004); Cape Cod Cranberry Growers' Association, www.cranberries.org/consumers/health.html (Accessed 28 April, 2004); USDA National Nutrient Database for Standard Reference, www.nal.usda.gov/fnic/foodcomp/search/index.html (Accessed 28 April, 2004)

Cobblers
Crunches
Crisps

APPLE-CRANBERRY COBBLER

Serve with a scoop of cinnamon or vanilla ice cream.

1 cup all-purpose flour
½ cup wheat germ
1 teaspoon baking powder
¼ teaspoon salt

½ cup butter or margarine,
   softened
½ cup granulated sugar
1½ tablespoons milk
1 large egg

6 cups cooking apples,
   peeled, cored and sliced
2 cups fresh or frozen
   cranberries, partially thawed
1 cup brown sugar, packed
1 teaspoon pure vanilla extract
½ teaspoon ground cinnamon
2 teaspoons cornstarch
¼ cup water

Preheat oven to 350°.
In a bowl, mix first four ingredients; set aside.

In a bowl, beat butter, then gradually beat in granulated sugar until creamy.
Add milk and egg; beat well. Stir in flour mixture to form a batter; set aside.

In a large bowl, mix apples, cranberries, brown sugar, vanilla and cinnamon.
Mix cornstarch with water in a cup; stir into apple mixture. Spoon mixture into
a lightly greased 11x7x1½-inch glass baking dish. Drop batter by spoonfuls
over fruit mixture. Bake, uncovered 45–50 minutes or until golden. Serve
warm. Refrigerate leftovers.

Makes 8 servings.

BLUEBERRY-CRANBERRY COBBLER

Serve warm, plain or with vanilla ice cream.

2 cups granulated sugar
¼ cup cornstarch
2 cups blueberries, fresh or frozen
2 cups cranberries, fresh or frozen
2 tablespoons fresh orange juice
1 teaspoon pure vanilla extract

1 6-ounce can refrigerated buttermilk biscuits
2 tablespoon granulated sugar
½ teaspoon freshly grated orange peel

Preheat oven to 375°.
In a saucepan, over medium heat, bring first six ingredients to a boil, stirring constantly. Reduce heat; simmer until cranberries pop and sauce is thickened. Spoon mixture into a greased 8-inch square baking pan.

Separate refrigerated biscuits and cut each into quarters. Mix 2 tablespoons sugar and orange peel in a small bowl. Add biscuit quarters; toss to coat. Place over hot fruit mixture. Bake 12–17 minutes or until biscuits are deep golden brown. Refrigerate leftovers.

Makes 6 servings.

PEACH-CRANBERRY COBBLER

Dried cranberries add a special flavor to this peachy cobbler.

½ cup butter

1 15-ounce package cranberry quick bread & muffin mix
1 tablespoon grated orange peel
2 29-ounce cans peach slices in light syrup, drained;
   reserve 1 cup syrup
1 teaspoon pure vanilla extract
1 egg, slightly beaten
⅓ cup sweetened dried cranberries

⅓ cup granulated sugar, mixed with:
   ¼ teaspoon ground cinnamon
   1 tablespoon grated orange peel

Preheat oven to 375°.
Melt butter in a 13x9-inch baking pan placed in the oven; remove.

Combine bread mix, 1 tablespoon orange peel, reserved peach syrup, vanilla and egg. Stir with a spoon, until moistened, about 50–75 strokes. Drop mixture by tablespoonfuls over hot butter in pan; spread a little without stirring. Place peaches over mixture. Sprinkle with cranberries.

Sprinkle top with sugar-cinnamon mixture. Bake 50–60 minutes or until edges are deep golden brown. Remove from oven. Cool slightly before serving. Refrigerate leftovers.

Makes 8 servings.

PINEAPPLE-CRANBERRY COBBLER

A dollop of whipped cream will complete the treat!

1 20-ounce can pineapple chunks in juice, drained
1 16-ounce can whole berry cranberry sauce
1 cup blueberries, fresh or frozen
½ cup brown sugar, packed
1 teaspoon ground cinnamon
¼ teaspoon ground nutmeg

1 teaspoon pure vanilla extract

2 cups all-purpose baking mix
9 tablespoons whole milk
1 tablespoon granulated sugar

Preheat oven to 400°
In a medium saucepan, gently mix first six ingredients; cook over medium heat, stirring occasionally, until mixture comes to a boil. Stir in vanilla. Pour mixture into a lightly greased 2-quart baking dish.

Stir baking mix and milk with a fork until a soft dough forms. Drop dough by rounded tablespoonfuls on top of hot fruit mixture. Sprinkle with granulated sugar. Bake 20–25 minutes. Remove from oven; cool slightly before serving. Serve warm. Refrigerate leftovers.

Makes 6 servings.

RHUBARB-CRANBERRY COBBLER

Serve warm topped with vanilla ice cream in dessert bowls.

2 cups granulated sugar, divided
3½ tablespoons cornstarch
¼ teaspoon ground cinnamon
¼ teaspoon ground ginger
8 cups frozen rhubarb,
   do not thaw
1 cup fresh or frozen cranberries
¼ cup frozen cranberry juice
   cocktail concentrate, thawed

½ cup butter, softened
1 large egg
1 teaspoon pure vanilla extract
½ cup whole milk

1 cup all-purpose flour
1 teaspoon baking powder
¼ teaspoon salt

Preheat oven to 350°.
In a large bowl, mix 1 cup sugar, cornstarch, cinnamon and ginger. Stir in rhubarb, cranberries and concentrate. Spoon into a buttered 13x9x2-inch glass baking dish. Bake until bubbling, about 30 minutes.

In a bowl, beat butter and 1 cup sugar until blended. Beat in egg, vanilla and milk.

In a small bowl, mix flour, baking powder and salt; add to butter mixture and beat to blend. Drop batter by tablespoonfuls over hot fruit mixture. Bake until topping is golden and filling is bubbling, about 40–50 minutes. Remove from oven. Refrigerate leftovers.

Makes 8 servings.

CARAMEL CRANBERRY CRUNCH

Serve plain or top with vanilla ice cream.

2 cups all-purpose flour
2 cups quick-cooking oats
¾ cup granulated sugar, divided
½ cup brown sugar, packed
1 teaspoon ground cinnamon
½ teaspoon baking soda
1 cup butter, melted

1 12-ounce package fresh or frozen cranberries
1½ cups chopped pecans
1 cup caramel ice cream topping

Preheat oven to 350°.
Combine flour, oats, ½ cup granulated sugar, brown sugar, cinnamon and baking soda in a large bowl. Stir in melted butter just until moistened; reserve 1 cup crumb mixture.

Press remaining crumb mixture onto bottom of an ungreased 15x10x1-inch jelly roll pan. Bake 15 minutes. Remove from oven; sprinkle crust with cranberries and pecans. Sprinkle with remaining granulated sugar. Drizzle with ice cream topping. Spoon reserved crumb mixture over top. Return to oven; bake 30–35 minutes or until golden. Remove from oven. Cool before cutting. Refrigerate leftovers.

Makes 24 servings.

THE GIRLS' CRANBERRY CRUNCH

A quick and easy dessert…top with vanilla ice cream when serving.

1½ cups rolled oats
½ cup all-purpose flour
¾ cup brown sugar
¼ teaspoon ground cinnamon
⅓ cup butter or margarine
1 16-ounce can jellied or whole berry cranberry sauce

Preheat oven to 350°.
In a bowl, mix oats, flour, sugar and cinnamon. Cut in butter until crumbly.
Spread half the mixture into a greased 8-inch square baking dish. Spread
with cranberry sauce. Top with remaining crumb mixture. Bake 45 minutes.
Serve warm. Refrigerate leftovers.

Makes 8 servings.

APPLE-APRICOT-CRANBERRY CRUMBLE

Apple cider, fresh apples, dried apricot and dried cranberries in this honey of a crumble.

1¾ cups apple cider
¼ cup finely chopped
   dried apricots
¼ cup sweetened
   dried cranberries

½ cup nutlike cereal
   nuggets (such as Grape-Nuts)
½ cup brown sugar,
   packed, divided

5 tablespoons all-purpose
   flour, divided
1 teaspoon ground
   cinnamon, divided
3 tablespoons honey
1 teaspoon pure vanilla extract
5 medium apples, peeled, cored
   and each cut into 8 wedges

Preheat oven to 350°.
Bring cider to a boil in a saucepan; remove from heat and stir in apricots and cranberries. Let stand 20 minutes; drain, reserving cider.

In a bowl, mix apricots, cranberries, cereal, ¼ cup brown sugar, 1 tablespoon flour and ½ teaspoon cinnamon.

In a large bowl, mix ¼ cup brown sugar, remaining 4 tablespoons flour and ½ teaspoon cinnamon. Stir in reserved cider, honey and vanilla. Add apples; toss to coat. Pour mixture in a buttered 11x7x1½-inch baking dish. Top evenly with apricot-cranberry-cereal mixture. Bake about 55 minutes. Remove from oven. Serve warm. Refrigerate leftovers.

Makes 6 servings.

FRESH CRANBERRY-APPLE CRISP

One of my husband's favorite desserts.

4 Golden Delicious apples, peeled, cored and coarsely chopped
2 cups fresh cranberries
1 cup granulated sugar
1½ teaspoons fresh lemon juice
½ teaspoon pure vanilla extract

1 cup quick-cooking oats
½ cup all-purpose flour
1 cup pecans coarsely chopped
½ cup butter, melted
⅓ cup brown sugar, packed

Preheat oven to 325°.
Mix apples and cranberries in a greased 11x7x2-inch baking dish. Sprinkle with sugar, lemon juice and vanilla.

In a bowl, mix remaining ingredients; sprinkle over fruit. Bake 1 hour or until golden. Serve warm with vanilla ice cream. Refrigerate leftovers.

Makes 8 servings.

PEAR-CRANBERRY CRISP

Serve warm with ice cream.

5 cups pears, peeled, cored and sliced (about 3 large pears)
1 cup cranberries, fresh or frozen
1 cup granulated sugar, divided
½ teaspoon pure vanilla extract

¾ cup all-purpose flour
½ teaspoon ground nutmeg
¼ teaspoon salt
½ cup butter or margarine, cup up
1 cup walnuts, coarsely chopped
½ cup rolled oats

Preheat oven to 350°.
Mix pears and cranberries in a greased, shallow 1½-quart baking dish.
Sprinkle with 3 tablespoons sugar; drizzle with vanilla.

In a large bowl, mix ¾ cup sugar, flour, nutmeg and salt. Cut in butter with pastry blender until mixture resembles coarse meal. Mix in walnut and oats. Sprinkle evenly over fruit. Bake about 40 minutes or until fruit is bubbly and top is lightly browned. Serve warm. Refrigerate leftovers.

Makes 6 servings.

Cakes
Coffeecakes
Cheesecakes

APPLESAUCE CRANBERRY CAKE

Applesauce and cranberry frosted cake...easy to prepare.

1 box (18.25-ounce) white cake mix
3 egg whites
1¼ cups water
¼ cup applesauce

Frosting
1 8-ounce package cream cheese, softened
¼ cup granulated sugar
1 8-ounce container frozen non-dairy whipped topping, thawed
1 16-ounce can whole berry cranberry sauce

Preheat oven to 350°.
Grease and lightly flour two 9-inch round baking pans.

In a large bowl, on low speed, mix cake mix, egg whites, water and applesauce until just combined, then on medium speed, beat 2 minutes. Pour batter into prepared pans. Bake 30–35 minutes or until a wooden pick inserted in center comes out clean. Cool in pans on a wire rack 10 minutes, then remove from pan and cool completely on rack.

Frosting: In a bowl, beat cream cheese, sugar and half of the whipped topping until smooth. Fold in cranberry sauce and remaining whipped topping. Chill frosting. Frost top of cooled cake. Store in refrigerator.

Makes 12 servings.

COCONUT CRANBERRY LAYER CAKE

A made from scratch layer cake.

Batter
1¼ cups butter, softened
1 cup granulated sugar
5 large eggs
3 cups cake flour, mixed with
    1 tablespoon baking powder
    and 1 teaspoon salt
1 cup whole milk, mixed with
    ½ cup water and 2 teaspoons
    pure vanilla extract

Filling
3½ cups fresh cranberries
1¼ cups granulated sugar
1 cup water
1 teaspoon pure vanilla extract

Frosting
2 large egg whites
1 cup granulated sugar
⅓ cup water
¼ teaspoon cream of tartar
1 7-ounce bag sweetened
    shredded coconut

Preheat oven to 350°.
Butter three 8-inch round cake pans and line bottoms with waxed paper;
butter and dust with flour; tap out excess.

Batter: Beat butter on medium speed 1 minute. Gradually beat in sugar
until fluffy, about 2 minutes. Beat in eggs one at a time. On low speed,
beat in flour and milk mixtures alternately, just until combined. Divide batter
among prepared pans. Bake 30 minutes or until wooden pick inserted in
center comes out clean. Invert layers onto a rack; remove paper; cool.

Filling: Bring cranberries, sugar and water to a boil; reduce heat and simmer,
stirring occasionally, 10 minutes. Stir in vanilla; cool to room temperature.

Frosting: In top of a double boiler, whisk frosting ingredients until sugar is
dissolved. With a hand-held mixer, beat frosting on high until thick and
fluffy, about 7 minutes. Remove from heat and beat until cool. Cut cake
layers horizontally in half. Place one layer cut side up on a plate; spread
with ½ cup filling. Repeat, ending with a cut-side down layer. Frost the cake
and apply coconut all over. Refrigerate leftovers.

Makes 10 servings.

CRANBERRY ANGEL FOOD CAKE

Serve plain or with a scoop of vanilla ice cream.

**1½ cups egg whites, room temperature
    (takes about 1 dozen eggs)
1¼ teaspoon cream of tartar
½ teaspoon salt
1½ cups granulated sugar, divided
1 cup plus 2 tablespoons
   sifted cake flour
1 teaspoon pure vanilla extract
zest of 1 fresh orange
1 cup fresh whole cranberries**

Preheat oven to 375°.
Whip egg whites until foamy. Add cream of tartar and salt, continue whipping until soft peaks form. Gradually add 1 cup sugar, and continue whipping until stiff and sugar has dissolved, about 30 seconds.

Sift remaining ½ cup sugar with pre-sifted cake flour three times. Fold into egg whites, then fold in vanilla, orange zest and cranberries. Spoon batter into an ungreased tube baking pan. Bake 30–35 minutes, until light golden brown. Remove from oven. Cool upside-down in pan to room temperature. Run a knife around cake to loosen, then remove cake from pan onto a plate. Pour glaze over top of cake; spread with a spatula, letting glaze trickle down sides.

Glaze: Stir melted butter and powdered sugar in a bowl. Stir in vanilla and add enough hot juice until smooth and to a desired consistency.

Makes 10 servings.

CRANBERRY CAKE

A family favorite from Cambridge, Minnesota...thanks Kathy.

1 cup all-purpose flour, sifted
1 teaspoon baking powder
½ cup granulated sugar
½ cup milk
1½ tablespoons melted butter
1 cup cranberries, halved

Sauce
¼ cup butter
1 cup granulated sugar
¾ cup heavy cream
1 teaspoon pure vanilla extract

Glaze
⅓ cup butter, melted
2 cups powdered sugar
1 teaspoon pure vanilla extract
2–4 tablespoons hot cranberry
juice or hot orange juice

Preheat oven to 350°.
Sift first three ingredients together in a bowl; add milk. Stir in melted butter and cranberries. Pour into greased and floured 8-inch pie plate or an 8-inch square cake pan. Bake 30 minutes. Remove from oven.

Sauce: Brown butter lightly in a skillet over medium heat; slowly add sugar, stirring constantly. Add cream and vanilla; bring to a boil. Pour warm sauce over cake.

Makes 8 servings.

CRANBERRY FRUITCAKE

Cranberries, raisins and walnuts in this tasty fruitcake.

1¼ cups granulated sugar
1 cup butter, softened
5 large eggs
½ cup brandy
1 tablespoon pure vanilla extract
2 cups all-purpose flour mixed
   with 2 teaspoons baking
   powder and 1 teaspoon salt

2 cups walnuts, toasted and
   coarsely chopped, mixed
   in a bowl with 1½ cups
   golden raisins, 1 cup dried
   cranberries and 1 tablespoon
   all-purpose flour
¾ cup walnut halves, toasted
⅓ cup apple jelly

Preheat oven to 325°.
Grease a 9-inch tube baking pan with removable bottom.

In a large bowl, beat sugar and butter on low speed until blended, then beat on high speed 2 minutes. On low speed, beat in eggs, brandy, vanilla and flour mixture until well blended. Stir in walnut-raisin mixture. Spoon batter into prepared pan.

Top with ¾ cup walnut halves. Bake about 1 hour and 15 minutes or until a wooden pick inserted in center comes out clean. Remove from oven; cool in pan 10 minutes. Run a small metal spatula around cake to loosen from side of pan. Invert cake onto wire rack; cool completely. Melt apple jelly, and brush over cake. Refrigerate.

Makes 24 servings.

CRANBERRY UPSIDE-DOWN CAKE

Serve plain or with whipped topping.

1 tablespoon margarine, melted
½ cup firmly packed brown
  sugar
2 cups cranberries

1½ cups sifted cake flour
1½ teaspoons baking powder
1 teaspoon ground cinnamon
¾ cup buttermilk

¼ cup stick margarine, softened
1 cup granulated sugar
2 large eggs
1½ teaspoons pure vanilla extract

Preheat oven to 350°.
Pour 1 tablespoon melted margarine in the bottom of a 9-inch springform baking pan. In a bowl, mix brown sugar with cranberries; arrange in a single layer over margarine.

Beat ¼ cup stick margarine, and 1 cup granulated sugar until well blended. Beat in eggs one at a time. Beat in vanilla.

In a bowl, mix cake flour, baking powder and cinnamon. Add to creamed mixture alternately with buttermilk. Spoon batter evenly over cranberries. Bake 45 minutes or until a wooden pick inserted in center comes out clean. Invert cake onto a serving plate. Refrigerate leftovers.

Makes 8 servings.

MOIST CRANBERRY POUND CAKE

Cranberry pound cake with warm sauce.

1 package (18.25-ounce)
  moist yellow cake mix
1 package (4-serving size)
  vanilla instant pudding
  & pie filling mix
1 cup water
½ cup butter, melted
1 teaspoon grated fresh orange peel
½ teaspoon pure vanilla extract
4 large eggs
1½ cups fresh cranberries, chopped

Sauce
1 cup granulated sugar
1 tablespoon all-purpose flour
½ cup fresh orange juice
½ cup butter, cut up
1 tablespoon dried
  sweetened cranberries
½ teaspoon pure vanilla extract

Preheat oven to 350°.
Beat dry cake mix, dry pudding mix, water, butter, orange peel, vanilla and
eggs on low speed 30 seconds, then beat 2 minutes on medium speed.
Fold in chopped cranberries. Spoon batter into a greased and floured
12-cup bundt cake pan. Bake 65–70 minutes or until cake springs back
when touched in center. Cool in pan 15 minutes. Remove from pan. Cool
completely. Serve warm with sauce.

Sauce: Mix sugar and flour in a saucepan. Stir in orange juice. Add butter.
Cook over medium heat, stirring constantly, until mixture thickens and is
bubbly. Stir in dried cranberries and vanilla. Refrigerate leftovers.

Makes 16 servings.

SNACKING CRANBERRY CAKE

It's snacking good.

½ cup butter, softened
1 cup granulated sugar
2 eggs
1 teaspoon pure vanilla extract

1½ cups all-purpose flour
2 teaspoons baking powder
½ teaspoon salt
¾ cup whole milk
1½ cups raw cranberries,
    chopped

Topping
1½ cups miniature marshmallows
½ cup brown sugar, packed
½ cup chopped pecans
2 tablespoons butter, melted

Preheat oven to 350°.
Beat butter and sugar until creamy. Beat in eggs and vanilla.

In another bowl, mix flour, baking powder and salt; add to creamed mixture
alternately with milk. Stir in cranberries. Pour into a greased 13x9x2-inch
baking pan.

Topping: Sprinkle top with marshmallows; press lightly into batter. Sprinkle
with brown sugar and pecans. Drizzle evenly with melted butter. Bake
35–40 minutes or until wooden pick inserted in center comes out clean.

Makes 12 servings.

SOUR CREAM CRANBERRY POUND CAKE

Serve plain, or with sweetened whipped cream.

1 cup butter, softened
2 cups granulated sugar, divided
1 tablespoon grated orange peel
6 large eggs, separated
1 cup dairy sour cream
1½ teaspoons pure vanilla extract

3 cups all-purpose flour
½ teaspoon baking soda

½ teaspoon salt
2¼ cups fresh or frozen
    cranberries, coarsely chopped

Glaze
⅓ cup granulated sugar
⅓ cup fresh orange juice
½ teaspoon vanilla extract

Preheat oven to 350°.
Grease and flour a 10-inch bundt cake pan.
Beat butter until creamy. Gradually beat in 1¾ cups sugar until light and fluffy. Beat in orange peel. Beat in egg yolks one at a time. Beat in sour cream and vanilla.

In another bowl, mix flour, soda and salt; using low speed, gradually beat into creamed mixture until just combined.

Beat egg whites in another bowl until foamy. Gradually add ¼ cup sugar, and beat until stiff peaks form; fold into batter (batter will be thick). Fold in cranberries. Spoon batter into prepared pan. Bake about 70 minutes or until a wooden pick inserted in center comes out clean. Cool in pan on a wire rack 15 minutes. Invert cake onto wire rack. Brush warm cake with warm glaze. Refrigerate leftovers.

Glaze: Simmer sugar and juice until sugar dissolves; stir in vanilla.

Makes 16 servings.

BREAD MACHINE CRANBERRY COFFEECAKE

Decorate glazed coffeecake with whole cranberries, fresh orange slices and toasted pecan halves.

Dough
½ **cup milk**
1 **large egg**
¼ **cup butter or margarine, cut up**
½ **teaspoon salt**
2½ **cups bread flour**
¼ **cup granulated sugar**
2 **teaspoons bread machine yeast**

Filling
1 **cup fresh or frozen cranberries, finely chopped**
⅔ **cup packed brown sugar**
¼ **cup butter**
½ **cup toasted chopped pecans**

Glaze
2 **tablespoons butter, softened**
1½ **cups powdered sugar**
1 **teaspoon pure vanilla extract**
2–3 **tablespoons orange juice, or as needed**

Dough: Add all dough ingredients to bread machine pan in order suggested by manufacturer. Select dough/manual cycle. In the meantime, prepare filling. When cycle is complete, roll dough out to a 26x6-inch rectangle on a floured surface; spread with filling to within ½-inch of edges. Beginning at long end, roll up tightly jelly roll style. Pinch seam to seal. Form into ring; join ends, pinching to seal. Place on a large greased baking sheet. Cover and let rise in a warm place, until doubled in size, about 45–60 minutes.

Filling: Bring cranberries, brown sugar and butter to a boil. Reduce heat; simmer 6 minutes or until thick, stirring often. Stir in pecans.

Preheat oven to 350°.
Bake 30–35 minutes or until done. Remove from baking sheet; cool on a wire rack. Drizzle with glaze.

Glaze: Mix all ingredients until smooth.

Makes 8 servings.

CRANBERRY LOAF COFFEECAKE

Serve cake warm or at room temperature.

2 cups fresh cranberries
1¾ cups granulated
**   sugar, divided**
½ cup butter, softened
2 large eggs
1 teaspoon pure vanilla extract

2 cups all-purpose flour
2 teaspoons baking powder
¾ teaspoon salt
½ cup whole milk

powdered sugar

Preheat oven to 350°.
Place cranberries and ½ cup sugar in food processor; pulse until finely chopped, but do not purée. Drain in a sieve.

Beat butter and remaining sugar until light and fluffy, about 5 minutes. Beat in eggs, one at a time. Beat in vanilla.

In a bowl, mix together flour, baking powder and salt. Using low speed, add to creamed mixture alternately with milk, mixing just until incorporated.

Spread one third of the batter into a well-buttered 9x5x3-inch loaf pan. Spoon half of the drained cranberries evenly over batter, leaving a ½-inch border along sides. Top with another third of batter, then remaining cranberries, again leaving ½-inch border along sides. Cover with remaining batter. Bake about 1 hour and 15 minutes or until a wooden pick inserted in center comes out clean. Remove from oven; cool in pan on a rack 30 minutes. Invert cake onto rack. Dust with powdered sugar.

Makes 8 servings.

CRANBERRY SWIRL COFFEECAKE

A slice of this cake with steaming coffee…nice breakfast treat.

½ cup butter
1 cup granulated sugar
2 eggs
1 teaspoon almond extract

2 cups all-purpose flour
1 teaspoon baking powder
1 teaspoon baking soda
½ teaspoon salt
1 cup dairy sour cream
1 8-ounce can whole cranberry sauce

Preheat oven to 350°.
Grease and flour a 9- or 10-inch tube baking pan.
In a large bowl, beat butter and sugar until light and fluffy. Beat in eggs, one at a time. Stir in almond extract.

In another bowl, mix flour, baking powder, baking soda and salt. Stir into creamy mixture alternately with sour cream. Pour a third of the batter into prepared baking pan. Swirl half of the cranberry sauce into batter. Repeat, ending with batter on top. Bake about 55 minutes or until tests done.

Makes 14 servings.

APPLESAUCE CRANBERRY CHEESECAKE

Cheesecake with a delicious sauce.

Crust
1¼ cups graham cracker crumbs
½ cup finely chopped
**   toasted pecans**
¼ cup brown sugar, packed
¼ cup butter, melted and cooled

Filling
3 8-ounce packages cream
**   cheese, softened**
1 cup granulated sugar
2 tablespoons all-purpose flour
3 eggs
1 cup applesauce
½ cup sweetened dried cranberries
1 teaspoon pure vanilla extract
¾ teaspoon ground cinnamon
pinch of ground nutmeg

Sauce
½ cup butter
1¼ cups brown sugar
2 tablespoons corn syrup
½ cup whipping cream
½ teaspoon pure vanilla extract
¾ cup toasted pecans
¼ cup sweetened dried
**   cranberries**

Preheat oven to 350°.
Crust: Mix all crust ingredients in a bowl; press into bottom of a 10-inch springform pan. Chill.

Filling: Beat cream cheese, granulated sugar and flour until fluffy. Beat in eggs one at a time. Add remaining filling ingredients; beat until well blended. Pour into prepared crust. Bake 50–60 minutes or until center is set. Cool 30 minutes, then refrigerate and chill well. Remove rim.

Sauce: Bring butter, brown sugar and corn syrup to a boil, stirring constantly. Gradually stir in cream; return to a boil. Remove from heat; stir in vanilla, pecans and cranberries. Top each serving with sauce. Refrigerate leftovers.

Makes 12 servings.

FESTIVE CRANBERRY CHEESECAKE

Make this cheesecake for special holiday dinners.

Cranberry mixture
1 cup granulated sugar
2 tablespoons cornstarch
1 cup cranberry juice
**1½ cups fresh or frozen
  cranberries**

Crust
1 cup graham cracker crumbs
3 tablespoons granulated sugar
⅛ teaspoon ground nutmeg
3 tablespoons butter, melted

Filling
**4 8-ounce packages
  cream cheese, softened**
1 cup granulated sugar
3 tablespoons all-purpose flour
4 eggs
1 cup commercial eggnog
1 tablespoon pure vanilla extract

Preheat oven to 325°.
Cranberry mixture: Bring all ingredients to a boil; reduce heat; cook and stir over medium heat 2 minutes. Remove from heat; set aside.

Crust: Mix all crust ingredients; press onto bottom of a greased 9-inch springform pan. Bake 8 minutes; cool on a wire rack.

Filling: Beat cream cheese and sugar until smooth. Beat in flour until well blended. Beat in eggs on low speed just until combined. Beat in eggnog and vanilla just until blended. Pour two-thirds of mixture over crust. Top with half of cranberry mixture (refrigerate the remaining half). Spoon remaining filling on top.

Bake 60–70 minutes or until center is almost set. Cool in pan on a wire rack 10 minutes. Run a knife around edge of pan to loosen; cool 1 hour longer, then refrigerate overnight. Before serving, remove sides of pan and spoon remaining cranberry mixture on top. Refrigerate leftovers.

Makes 12 servings.

ORANGE-CRANBERRY CHEESECAKE

Use frozen cranberries when fresh are not available.

Crust
- 1½ cups crushed vanilla wafer crumbs
- 3 tablespoons finely chopped walnuts
- ¼ cup butter, melted and slightly cooled

Topping
- ½ cup frozen cranberry juice cocktail concentrate, thawed
- 6 tablespoons orange marmalade
- 1 teaspoon fresh lemon juice
- 1 teaspoon finely shredded fresh orange peel

Filling
- 3 8-ounce packages cream cheese, softened
- ¾ cup granulated sugar
- 5 teaspoons cornstarch
- 3 eggs plus 1 egg yolk
- ½ cup frozen cranberry juice cocktail concentrate, thawed
- 1 teaspoon finely shredded fresh orange peel
- 1 teaspoon pure vanilla extract
- 1 cup fresh cranberries, finely chopped
- ⅓ cup finely chopped walnuts

Crust: Mix all crust ingredients; press mixture into bottom of a greased 9-inch springform pan.

Filling: Beat cream cheese until fluffy; beat in sugar and cornstarch until smooth. Beat in eggs one at a time. Beat in egg yolk. Add cranberry concentrate, orange peel and vanilla; beat until blended. Stir in cranberries and walnuts. Pour over prepared crust. Bake 15 minutes. Reduce heat to 300°. Bake 60–70 minutes or until center is almost set. Cool 10 minutes, then run a knife around edges of pan to loosen. Refrigerate uncovered 8 hours. Remove sides from pan before serving.

Topping: Stir all ingredients over medium heat until bubbly and thick; cool slightly. Spoon over cheesecake when serving. Refrigerate leftovers.

Makes 12 servings.

SAM'S CRANBERRY CHEESECAKE

An ultimate cheesecake…like Sam, unforgettable.

Crust
**2 cups finely ground graham
   crackers**
½ teaspoon ground cinnamon
1 stick unsalted butter, melted

Filling
2 8-ounce packages cream cheese, softened
3 eggs
1 cup granulated sugar
2 cups dairy sour cream
1 teaspoon pure vanilla extract
1 teaspoon fresh lemon zest

Topping
**½ cup granulated sugar mixed
   with 1 teaspoon cornstarch**
¼ cup water
2 cups fresh cranberries
½ teaspoon grated orange peel

Preheat oven to 325°.
Lightly butter sides and bottom of an 8-inch springform pan.

Crust: Mix all crust ingredients; press onto bottom and 1-inch up sides of prepared pan; refrigerate.

Filling: Beat cream cheese on medium until smooth, about 1 minute. Beat in eggs one at a time. Gradually beat in sugar. Beat in remaining ingredients until creamy. Pour into prepared crust. Place pan on heavy aluminum foil, folding sides around it (not the top). Place in a larger pan and fill that pan with boiling water about halfway up the sides (the foil will keep the water from seeping into the cheesecake). Bake 45–70 minutes or until center is almost set, but still has a little jiggle. Cool in pan 30 minutes, then refrigerate and chill loosely covered for 4 hours or more. Run a thin knife around sides to loosen; remove rim. Spread with cranberry topping.

Topping: Cook and stir all topping ingredients until cranberries pop. Chill well. Refrigerate leftovers.

Makes 8 servings.

SWEET POTATO CRANBERRY CHEESECAKE

Sweet potatoes, cranberries and cream cheese in a gingersnap-pecan crust...yummy.

Crust
1 cup gingersnap cookie crumbs
½ cup finely chopped pecans
3 tablespoons butter, melted
** and slightly cooled**

Topping
miniature marshmallows
sweetened dried cranberries
toasted pecan halves

Filling
2 8-ounce packages cream cheese, softened
½ cup granulated sugar, mixed with 1 teaspoon ground cinnamon
2 eggs
1 17-ounce can sweet potatoes, well drained
¼ cup orange juice
½ cup dairy sour cream
1 teaspoon pure vanilla extract
½ cup sweetened dried cranberries

Preheat oven to 325°.
Crust: Mix all crust ingredients; press onto bottom of a 9-inch springform pan.

Filling: Beat cream cheese and sugar mixture until fluffy. Beat in eggs. Add remaining ingredients; beat on low speed until blended. Pour into prepared crust. Bake 1 hour. Loosen cake from rim of pan. Cool 30 minutes; remove rim. Refrigerate and chill.

Topping: Just before serving, top with marshmallows; broil until lightly browned. Garnish with cranberries and pecan halves. Refrigerate leftovers.

Makes 12 servings.

WHITE CHOCOLATE CRANBERRY CHEESECAKE

Garnish with whipped topping and additional sweetened dried cranberries when serving.

Crust
1¼ cups créme-filled chocolate sandwich cookie crumbs
¼ cup butter, melted and cooled slightly

Filling
3 8-ounce packages cream cheese, softened
¾ cup granulated sugar
3 large eggs
4 ounces white baking chocolate, melted
½ cup sweetened dried cranberries
1 teaspoon freshly grated orange peel
1 teaspoon pure vanilla extract

Preheat oven to 350°
Crust: Mix crust ingredients in a bowl; press onto bottom of a 9-inch springform pan. Chill.

Filling: Beat cream cheese on medium speed until fluffy. Beat in sugar until blended. Beat in eggs until blended. Stir in white chocolate, cranberries, orange peel and vanilla. Pour into prepared crust. Bake 45–50 minutes or until center is almost set. Cool in pan 30 minutes, then refrigerate. Run a knife around sides of pan to loosen. Chill 4 hours or more. Remove rim; cut into wedges. Refrigerate leftovers.

Makes 12 servings.

Bars
Squares
Cookies

APPLESAUCE CRANBERRY BARS

Fresh or frozen cranberries may be used for these bars.

6 tablespoons butter
¾ cup brown sugar, packed
½ cup applesauce
1 egg, beaten
1 teaspoon grated orange peel
1 teaspoon pure vanilla extract

Dry ingredients
1¼ cups all-purpose flour
1 teaspoon baking powder
¼ teaspoon baking soda

1 cup chopped raw cranberries
½ cup chopped pecans

powdered sugar

Preheat oven to 350°.
Stir butter and sugar in a saucepan until butter just melts. Remove from heat; stir in applesauce, egg, orange peel and vanilla until well blended.

Mix dry ingredients; stir into applesauce mixture; stir in cranberries and pecans. Spread mixture into a 9-inch baking pan coated with cooking spray. Bake 25 minutes. Cool in pan on a wire rack. Sprinkle with powdered sugar as desired. Refrigerate leftovers.

Makes 24 bars.

CHOCOLATE CAKE MIX CRANBERRY BARS

Caramels and cranberries in this chocolate bar.

1 14-ounce package vanilla caramels, unwrapped
⅔ cup half & half (light cream), divided
1 package (2-layer size) German chocolate cake mix
¼ cup melted butter
1 teaspoon pure vanilla extract
1 16-ounce can whole berry cranberry sauce
½ cup chopped pecans

Preheat oven to 350°.
In a heavy saucepan, heat caramels and ⅓ cup half & half over low heat, stirring occasionally, until caramels are melted; stir until smooth. Remove from heat.

Beat cake mix, remaining ⅓ cup half & half, butter and vanilla until smooth. Pat half the mixture in bottom of a greased 13x9x2-inch baking pan. Bake 10 minutes; remove from oven. Spread evenly with warm caramel mixture. Stir cranberry sauce in a bowl, and spoon over caramel layer. Sprinkle remaining cake mixture over cranberry layer. Sprinkle with pecans. Return to oven; bake 30 minutes. Cool in pan on a wire rack. Cut into bars.

Makes 20 bars.

CHOCOLATE CHIP CRANBERRY
CREAM CHEESE BARS

Chocolate chips, cranberry and cream cheese…a tasty treat.

1 cup butter or margarine, softened
1 cup brown sugar, packed
2 cups all-purpose flour
1½ cups quick-cooking oats
2 teaspoons grated orange peel
2 cups semi-sweet chocolate chips
1 cup sweetened dried cranberries

1 8-ounce package cream cheese, softened
1 14-ounce can sweetened condensed milk (not evaporated)
1 teaspoon pure vanilla extract

Preheat oven to 350°.
Beat butter and sugar until creamy. Gradually beat in flour, oats and orange peel until crumbly. Stir in chocolate chips and cranberries; reserve 2 cups mixture. Press remaining mixture onto bottom of a greased 13x9-inch baking pan. Bake 15 minutes. Remove from oven.

Beat cream cheese until smooth. Gradually beat in sweetened condensed milk. Beat in vanilla. Pour mixture over hot crust; sprinkle with reserved mixture. Return to oven; bake 25–30 minutes or until center is set. Cool in pan on a wire rack. Cut into bars. Refrigerate leftovers.

Makes 36 bars.

CHOCOLATE PEANUT BUTTER CRANBERRY BARS

Yummy.

2 cups vanilla wafer crumbs
½ cup unsweetened cocoa powder
3 tablespoons granulated sugar
⅔ cup cold butter, cut up

1 14-ounce can sweetened condensed milk (not evaporated)
1 teaspoon pure vanilla extract
1 cup peanut butter chips
1⅓ cups sweetened dried cranberries
1 cup coarsely chopped walnuts

Preheat oven to 350°.
Stir together crumbs, cocoa and sugar; cut in butter until mixture is crumbly. Press mixture onto bottom and ½-inch up sides of a 13x9x2-inch baking pan.

Pour sweetened condensed milk evenly over crumb mixture; drizzle evenly with vanilla. Sprinkle evenly with peanut butter chips, cranberries and walnuts. Press down firmly. Bake 25–30 minutes or until lightly browned. Cool completely in pan on a wire rack. Cover with cooking foil and let stand several hours. Cut into bars.

Makes 36 bars.

COCONUT CRANBERRY BARS

Coconut and cranberries in this sweet bar.

1½ cups all-purpose flour
¾ cup granulated sugar
¾ cup cold butter

Filling:
2 cups sweetened flaked coconut
1 cup sweetened dried cranberries
¾ cup brown sugar, packed
⅓ cup all-purpose flour
3 eggs
1½ teaspoons pure vanilla extract
¼ teaspoon salt

Preheat oven to 350°.
Mix flour and granulated sugar; cut in butter until mixture resembles coarse crumbs. Press mixture onto bottom of an ungreased 13x9-inch baking pan. Bake 15 minutes or until edges are lightly browned.

Filling: Mix all ingredients until well blended. Spread filling over hot, partially baked crust. Return to oven; bake 25–30 minutes or until golden brown. Cool completely in pan on a wire rack. Cut into bars. Refrigerate leftovers.

Makes 36 bars.

CRANBERRY CREAM CHEESE BARS

Good treat for an afternoon tea.

Crust
1 package (18.25-ounce) moist yellow cake mix
½ cup butter or margarine, softened
1 egg
¼ cup chopped pecans

Filling
1 8-ounce package cream cheese, softened
¼ cup powdered sugar
1 egg
1 teaspoon pure vanilla extract
¼ teaspoon ground cinnamon
⅛ teaspoon ground nutmeg
1 10-ounce can whole berry cranberry sauce

Preheat oven to 350°.
Using an electric mixer, beat cake mix, butter and egg on low speed until crumbly. Stir in pecans. Press mixture evenly onto bottom of an ungreased 13x9x2-inch baking pan. Bake until crust is set but not browned, about 8–10 minutes.

Filling: Beat cream cheese and sugar until fluffy. Beat in egg, vanilla, cinnamon and nutmeg. Pour mixture over crust. Spoon cranberry sauce over mixture in three long rows, then swirl with a knife. Bake until set, about 30–40 minutes. Remove from oven; cool completely. Cut into bars. Store in refrigerator.

Makes 36 bars.

CRANBERRY-DATE BARS

An orange glaze completes this cranberry-date bar.

1 12-ounce package cranberries
1 8-ounce package chopped
    pitted dates
1 teaspoon pure vanilla extract

2 cups all-purpose flour
2 cups rolled oats
1½ cups brown sugar, packed
½ teaspoon baking soda
¼ teaspoon salt
1 cup butter, melted

Glaze
2 cups powdered sugar
½ teaspoon pure vanilla extract
2 tablespoons orange juice, or as
    needed

Preheat oven to 350°.
In a covered medium saucepan, cook cranberries and dates over low heat,
stirring often, 10–15 minutes or until cranberries pop. Remove from heat;
stir in vanilla.

Stir flour, oats, brown sugar, soda and salt. Add butter; stir until blended.
Pat half of mixture onto bottom of an ungreased 13x9x2-inch baking pan.
Bake 8 minutes. Remove from oven. Carefully spread filling over baked
mixture. Sprinkle remaining flour mixture on top; pat down gently. Return to
oven; bake 20–24 minutes or until golden. Cool completely in pan on a
wire rack. Drizzle with glaze.

Glaze: Mix ingredients to a loose drizzling consistency.

Make 32 bars.

CRANBERRY MACADAMIA BARS

A sweet orange glaze tops these delicious bars.

⅔ cup all-purpose flour
⅓ cup cold butter, cut up
2 tablespoons granulated sugar

Filling:
½ cup sweetened flaked coconut
⅔ cup macadamia nuts, coarsely chopped (3.25-ounce jar)
½ cup sweetened dried cranberries
⅓ cup granulated sugar
2 eggs, beaten
1 teaspoon pure vanilla extract
½ teaspoon baking powder
¼ teaspoon salt

Glaze:
1 cup powdered sugar
½ teaspoon pure vanilla extract
3 tablespoons orange juice, or as needed

Preheat oven to 350°.
Beat first three ingredients in a bowl on low speed until crumbly. Press mixture into an ungreased 8-inch square pan. Bake about 15 minutes or until lightly browned.

Mix all filling ingredients in a bowl until well blended. Spread evenly over hot, partially baked crust. Return to oven and bake about 25 minutes or until golden brown. Remove from oven and drizzle with glaze.

Glaze: Mix all glaze ingredients, using just enough orange juice to form a desired glaze. Drizzle over warm bars. Cool completely. Cut into bars.

Makes 25 bars.

CRANBERRY-PEACH CHEESE BARS

Cranberry-peach preserves top this delicious cream cheese bar.

2 cups all-purpose flour
¾ cup butter, softened
¼ cup granulated sugar
⅓ cup light corn syrup
½ teaspoon salt

2 8-ounce packages cream cheese, softened
3 eggs
1 cup light corn syrup
2 teaspoons pure vanilla extract
¾ cup cranberry-peach preserves

Preheat oven to 375°.
Beat flour, butter, sugar, ⅓ cup corn syrup and salt on low speed until a dough forms; press dough evenly into a greased 13x9x2-inch baking pan. Set aside.

Beat cream cheese until smooth; beat in eggs one at a time; beat in 1 cup corn syrup and vanilla until mixture is smooth. Pour over dough in prepared pan. Bake 35–40 minutes or until filling is set. Remove from oven and immediately spread preserves on top. Refrigerate and chill before cutting into bars. Store in refrigerator.

Makes 36 bars.

CRANBERRY TURTLE BARS

Cranberries, pecans and chocolate…a good bar.

Crust
- **2 cups all-purpose flour**
- **½ cup light brown sugar, packed**
- **½ teaspoon salt**
- **¾ cup cold butter, cut up**

Topping
- **1 cup butter**
- **1⅔ cups granulated sugar**
- **¼ cup light corn syrup**
- **½ teaspoon salt**
- **1½ cups fresh cranberries, coarsely chopped**
- **1 teaspoon pure vanilla extract**
- **3 cups pecans, toasted, cooled, coarsely chopped**

- **2 ounces bittersweet chocolate, finely chopped**

Preheat oven to 350°.
Line a 15x10x1-inch pan with foil, leaving a 2-inch overhang on the short sides. Butter all four sides, but not the bottom.

In a food processor, blend flour, brown sugar and salt. Add butter; pulse until mixture begins to form pea-size lumps. Place mixture in prepared pan; press down firmly with a metal spatula to form an even crust. Bake 15–17 minutes. Cool in pan on a wire rack.

Topping: Melt butter in a heavy 3-quart saucepan over medium heat. Stir in sugar, corn syrup and salt. Boil over medium-high heat, stirring occasionally, until a candy thermometer registers 245°, about 8 minutes. Stir in cranberries; boil until temperature returns to 245°. Remove from heat; stir in vanilla; quickly stir in pecans. Spread over crust. Cool completely in pan on a wire rack. Remove from foil to a cutting board. Cut into bars.

Melt chocolate; drizzle over bars. Let stand until chocolate sets. Refrigerate.

Makes 36 bars.

FROSTED CARROT-ZUCCHINI-CRANBERRY BARS

Tastes like carrot cake!

Bars
2 cups all-purpose flour
2 teaspoons baking powder
½ teaspoon baking soda
⅛ teaspoon salt
2 teaspoons finely
  shredded orange peel
3 eggs, beaten
1½ cups brown sugar, packed
⅔ cup corn oil
¼ cup milk
1½ teaspoons pure
  vanilla extract

1 cup finely shredded carrots
1 cup finely shredded,
  unpeeled zucchini
¾ cup coarsely chopped
  cranberries

Frosting
4 ounces cream cheese, softened
⅓ cup butter, softened
½ teaspoon pure vanilla extract
3 cups powdered sugar
4 teaspoons orange juice,
  or as needed

Preheat oven to 350°.
In a large bowl, mix first five ingredients. In another bowl, mix next five ingredients, then stir in carrots, zucchini and cranberries. Add mixture to flour mixture; stir until combined. Spread batter into a greased 15x10x1-inch baking pan. Bake 20–25 minutes or until a wooden pick inserted in center comes out clean. Cool in pan on a wire rack. Frost and store covered in refrigerator.

Frosting: Beat cream cheese and butter until smooth. Add vanilla. Gradually beat in powdered sugar and enough orange juice to form a spreading consistency. (Use immediately or refrigerate).

Makes 36 bars.

PINEAPPLE-CRANBERRY BARS

Pineapple and cranberries…a good combination.

1 cup fresh or frozen cranberries
3 tablespoons brown sugar
1½ teaspoon cornstarch
1 8-ounce can crushed pineapple, undrained

¾ cup all-purpose flour
¾ cup quick-cooking oats
¼ teaspoon ground cinnamon
¼ teaspoon ground ginger
3 tablespoons cold butter, cut up
3 tablespoons chopped pecans

Preheat oven to 350°.
Stir first four ingredients in a saucepan over medium heat; bring to a boil; cook 1 minute. Reduce heat; cover and simmer 12 minutes or until cranberries pop and mixture thickens, stirring occasionally. Set aside.

Mix flour, oats, cinnamon and ginger. Cut in butter with a pastry blender until mixture resembles coarse meal. Reserve ½ cup. Press remaining mixture into a greased 8-inch square baking pan. Bake 10 minutes. Remove from oven; spread pineapple-cranberry mixture over crust. Mix reserved oat mixture with pecans; sprinkle over last layer. Return to oven; bake 27 minutes. Cool in pan on a wire rack.

Makes 16 bars.

PUMPKIN-CRANBERRY BARS

A brown butter frosting adds a finishing touch to these bars.

Bars
1½ cups all-purpose flour
1¼ cups granulated sugar
2 teaspoons baking powder
¾ teaspoon baking soda
1½ teaspoons ground cinnamon
½ teaspoon ground ginger
⅛ teaspoon ground cloves
1 15-ounce can pumpkin purée
¾ cup butter, melted
3 large eggs
1 teaspoon pure vanilla extract
¾ cup chopped dried cranberries

Frosting
½ cup butter
4 cups powdered sugar
1 teaspoon pure
** vanilla extract**
⅓ cup pure orange juice,
** approximately**

Preheat oven to 350°.
In a large bowl, mix together first seven ingredients. Stir in pumpkin, butter, eggs and vanilla until well blended. Stir in cranberries. Spread mixture into an ungreased 15x10-inch jelly-roll baking pan. Bake 20–25 minutes or until a wooden pick inserted in center comes out clean. Cool completely in pan on a wire rack. Frost and cut into bars. Refrigerate leftovers.

Frosting: Melt butter in a saucepan over medium heat, stirring often, until butter just starts to turn to a golden color (do not let burn). Remove immediately from heat and pour into a bowl; cool slightly, then stir in powdered sugar and vanilla. Stir in enough orange juice to a form a frosting consistency.

Makes 36 bars.

SOUR CREAM CRANBERRY BARS

Sour cream adds a special flavor to this cranberry bar.

1 cup butter or margarine, softened
1 cup brown sugar, packed
2 cups quick-cooking oats
1½ cups all-purpose flour
1 teaspoon baking soda

2 cups dried sweetened cranberries
1 cup dairy sour cream
¾ cup granulated sugar
1 tablespoon grated lemon peel
1 teaspoon pure vanilla extract
1 egg, slightly beaten

Preheat oven to 350°.
Stir together butter and brown sugar with a spoon. In another bowl, stir oats, flour and baking soda; add to creamed mixture, stirring until crumbly. Press half the mixture in an ungreased 13x9x2-inch baking pan. Bake 10–12 minutes or until golden brown. Remove from oven.

Mix remaining ingredients; pour over hot crust. Crumble remaining oat mixture over filling. Return to oven; bake 25–30 minutes, or until top is golden brown and filling is set. Cool completely in pan on a wire rack. Cut into bars.

Makes 24 bars.

CRANBERRY CHEESE SQUARES

Garnish with sweetened whipped cream when serving.

2 cups all-purpose flour
1½ cups quick-cooking oats
1 cup butter or margarine, softened
¾ cup light brown sugar, packed

1 8-ounce package cream cheese, softened
1 14-ounce can sweetened condensed milk (not evaporated)
¼ cup lemon juice
1 teaspoon pure vanilla extract

1 16-ounce can whole berry cranberry sauce
2 tablespoons cornstarch, mixed with 1 tablespoon
   light brown sugar

Preheat oven to 350°.
Beat flour, oats, butter and brown sugar until crumbly. Reserve 1½ cups. Press remaining mixture firmly onto bottom of a greased 13x9-inch baking pan. Bake until lightly browned, about 15 minutes. Remove from oven; set aside.

Beat cream cheese until fluffy. Gradually beat in sweetened condensed milk; stir in lemon juice and vanilla. Spread over baked crust. In another bowl, stir cranberry sauce and cornstarch mixture until blended; spoon over cream cheese layer. Top with reserved crumb mixture. Bake 45 minutes. Cool; cut into squares. Store in refrigerator.

Makes 24 servings.

LEMON-CRANBERRY SQUARES

Dust these dessert squares with powdered sugar when serving.

1½ cups dried cranberries
2 cups cold water
¼ cup powdered sugar
1 cup all-purpose flour, divided
6 tablespoons cold butter, cut up

2 large eggs
¾ cup granulated sugar
½ teaspoon pure vanilla extract
¼ cup fresh lemon juice

Preheat oven to 325°.
Bring cranberries and water to a boil in a saucepan. Reduce heat; cook, stirring often, until water is absorbed, about 25 minutes. Coarsely chop cranberries in a food processor; set aside.

In a mixer bowl, using paddle attachment, mix powdered sugar and ¾ cup flour. Add butter; beat on low speed until pea-size lumps are formed. Press mixture into an 8-inch buttered baking pan. Bake about 20 minutes or until golden. Cool on a wire rack.

Beat eggs and granulated sugar until smooth; beat in vanilla and lemon juice. Beat in ¼ cup flour until combined.

Reduce heat to 300°. Spread cranberry mixture over baked crust. Pour lemon mixture over cranberry layer. Bake until set, about 40 minutes. Remove from oven; cool in pan on a wire rack, then refrigerate. Chill well before cutting into squares. Store in refrigerator.

Makes 16 servings.

MINCEMEAT CRANBERRY SQUARES

Mincemeat, cranberry and cream cheese in this festive square.

2 cups all-purpose flour
1½ cups quick-cooking oats
¾ cup brown sugar, packed
1 cup butter or margarine, softened

1 8-ounce package cream cheese, softened
1 14-ounce can sweetened condensed milk (not evaporated)
2 eggs
1 27-ounce jar ready-to-use mincemeat, regular or brandy & rum

2 tablespoons cornstarch, mixed with 1 tablespoon brown sugar
1 16-ounce can whole berry cranberry sauce

Preheat oven to 350°.
Beat flour, oats, ¾ cup sugar and butter until crumbly. Reserve 1½ cups; press remaining mixture onto bottom of a greased 15x10-inch jelly roll pan. Bake 15 minutes or until lightly browned. Set aside.

Beat cream cheese until fluffy. Gradually beat in sweetened condensed milk until smooth. Beat in eggs; spread mixture over baked crust. Top evenly with mincemeat.

Combine cornstarch mixture and cranberry sauce until combined; spoon over mincemeat layer. Top with reserved crumb mixture. Bake 40 minutes or until golden. Cool in pan on a wire rack. Chill, then cut into squares. Store in refrigerator.

Makes 16 servings.

CHOCOLATE CHIP CRANBERRY BISCOTTI

Delicious crunchy cookies…a good after-dinner treat.

2¾ cups all-purpose flour
1 cup granulated sugar
½ cup dried sweetened cranberries
⅓ cup semisweet chocolate chips
2 teaspoons baking powder
⅛ teaspoon salt

1 tablespoon vegetable oil
1 teaspoon pure vanilla extract
½ teaspoon almond extract
3 large eggs, beaten

Preheat oven to 350°.
In a large bowl, mix the first six ingredients.

In a small bowl, mix the remaining four ingredients; stir into the flour mixture until well blended. Knead dough on a lightly floured surface until smooth. Divide dough in half; shape each half into an 8-inch long log. Place logs 6-inches apart on a baking sheet coated with cooking spray, then flatten each to 1-inch thickness.

Bake 35 minutes. Remove logs from baking sheet; cool 10 minutes on a wire rack. Cut each diagonally into 15 half-inch size slices. Place slices cut side down on baking sheet. Reduce heat to 325°. Bake 10 minutes. Turn cookies over; bake an additional 10 minutes. Remove from baking sheet and cool completely on a wire rack.

Makes 2½ dozen.

CRANBERRY CORNMEAL COOKIES

Butter cookies with a hint of cornmeal and tangy cranberries.

¾ cup granulated sugar
¾ cup butter, softened
1 egg
1 tablespoon corn syrup
1 teaspoon pure vanilla extract
1½ cups all-purpose flour
½ cup yellow cornmeal
1 teaspoon baking powder
¼ teaspoon salt
¼ teaspoon ground cinnamon
¾ cup sweetened dried cranberries, chopped

granulated sugar in a bowl for rolling

Preheat oven to 350°.
Beat sugar and butter until creamy. Beat in egg, corn syrup and vanilla until well blended. In a small bowl, mix flour, cornmeal, baking powder, salt and cinnamon; beat into creamed mixture on low speed until well blended. By hand, stir in cranberries.

Form rounded teaspoonfuls of dough into balls; roll in sugar. Place balls 1 inch apart on an ungreased baking sheet; flatten slightly. Bake 9–12 minutes or until edges are lightly browned. Cool on a wire rack.

Makes 3½ dozen.

CRANBERRY PEANUT BUTTER THUMB PRINTS

Cranberry peanut butter thumb prints...kids will love them.

½ cup butter or margarine, softened
½ cup granulated sugar
½ cup brown sugar, packed
½ cup peanut butter
1 teaspoon pure vanilla extract
1 egg
1½ cups all-purpose flour, mixed with 1 teaspoon baking soda
1 16-ounce can jellied cranberry sauce, stirred until smooth

Preheat oven to 350°.
Beat butter and sugars until fluffy. Beat in peanut butter, vanilla and egg. Stir in flour mixture until well blended.

Roll dough into 1-inch balls. Place on baking sheets. Make an indent with thumb into the center of each ball. Spoon a scant teaspoon of cranberry sauce into the indent. Bake 15 minutes or until almost firm to touch. Cool on a wire rack.

Makes 3 dozen.

CRANBERRY SHORTBREAD

A delicate cookie.

2½ cups all-purpose flour
½ cup granulated sugar
¼ teaspoon salt
1 cup butter (no substitution)
½ cup very finely chopped dried cranberries

Preheat oven to 325°.
Stir together flour, sugar and salt. Cut in butter until mixture resembles fine crumbs. Stir in cranberries. Form into a ball and knead until smooth. Divide dough in half.

Pat or roll each dough portion on a lightly floured surface to a ½-inch thickness. Using a knife, cut into 24 2x1-inch strips. Place 1 inch apart on an ungreased baking sheet. Bake 20–25 minutes or until bottoms just start to brown. Cool on baking sheet 5 minutes, then remove and cool completely on a wire rack.

Makes 4 dozen strips.

MILK CHOCOLATE CRANBERRY COOKIES

For a firmer cookie, bake about 14 minutes.

1 11-ounce bag milk chocolate morsels, divided
½ cup brown sugar
¼ cup butter, softened
2 eggs
1 teaspoon pure vanilla extract
¾ cup all-purpose flour, mixed with ¼ teaspoon baking powder
1 6-ounce package cherry-flavor sweetened dried cranberries
1 cup pecans, coarsely chopped

Preheat oven to 350°.
In a large microwave-safe bowl, microwave ¾ cup chocolate morsels for
two minutes on high. Stir until chocolate is smooth.

Stir in sugar, butter, eggs and vanilla. Stir in flour mixture until blended.
Stir in remaining chocolate morsels, cranberries and pecans.

Drop by tablespoonfuls onto a greased baking sheet. Bake 12 minutes
or until cookies are puffed and set to touch. Remove from oven; cool on
baking sheet 2 minutes. Remove from baking sheet to a wire rack to cool.

Makes 2½ dozen.

ORANGE ALMOND CRANBERRY BISCOTTI

A great cookie for that coffee party.

1 cup granulated sugar
½ cup butter or margarine
2 eggs
1 tablespoon freshly grated orange zest
¼ teaspoon almond extract

3½ cups all-purpose flour
1 teaspoon baking powder
½ teaspoon salt
½ cup orange-flavor sweetened dried cranberries
⅓ cup slivered almonds, toasted and chopped

Preheat oven to 350°.
Beat sugar, butter, eggs, orange zest and almond extract until creamy.

In another bowl, mix flour, baking powder, salt, cranberries and almonds; add to creamed mixture; mix well.

Divide dough in half; shape each half into a 10x3-inch rectangle on an ungreased baking sheet. Bake 20 minutes or until a wooden pick inserted center comes out clean. Cool on baking sheet 15 minutes. Cut crosswise into ½-inch slices. Turn the slices cut side down on baking sheet. Bake an additional 15 minutes or until crisp and light brown. Remove from baking sheet; cool completely on a wire rack.

Makes 4 dozen.

ORANGE-CRANBERRY SPICE COOKIES

Sugar and spice…orange flavor, molasses and cranberries!

1 cup butter or margarine, softened
½ cup granulated sugar
1 cup brown sugar, packed
1 teaspoon pure vanilla extract
2 teaspoons finely grated fresh orange rind
2 teaspoons orange extract
1 large egg
½ cup molasses

2½ cups all-purpose flour
2 teaspoons baking powder
½ teaspoon salt
2 teaspoons ground cinnamon
1 teaspoon ground ginger
½ teaspoon ground cloves

1 cup dried cranberries

granulated sugar in a bowl for rolling

Preheat oven to 350°.
Beat butter and sugars until smooth. Add vanilla, orange rind and orange extract. Add egg and beat until fluffy. Pour in molasses; mix until fully incorporated.

In another bowl, sift flour and all dry ingredients; gradually beat into sugar mixture. Stir in cranberries. Place dough in freezer for 10 minutes. Form into balls the size of golf balls; roll in granulated sugar, and lightly flatten in palm of hand. Place on a greased or parchment-lined baking sheet. Bake 10–12 minutes. Remove from oven; cool cookies on baking sheet 7 minutes. Remove from baking sheet; cool completely on a wire rack.

Makes 3 dozen.

PECAN CRANBERRY JUMBLES

Cranberry pecan cookies…a good choice to bake for holiday gifts.

1 cup brown sugar, packed
½ cup butter, softened
½ cup dairy sour cream
1 egg
1 teaspoon pure vanilla extract

2 cups all-purpose flour
¾ teaspoon baking powder
¼ teaspoon baking soda
1 cup coarsely chopped pecans
1 6-ounce package sweetened dried cranberries

Icing
2 cups powdered sugar
3–4 tablespoons orange juice

Preheat oven to 375°.
Beat brown sugar, butter, sour cream, egg and vanilla in a large bowl on medium speed until creamy. Using low speed, beat in flour, baking powder and baking soda until well mixed. Stir in pecans and cranberries by hand. Drop dough by rounded teaspoonfuls 2 inches apart on an ungreased baking sheet. Bake 10–12 minutes or until lightly browned. Cool completely on a wire rack.

Icing: Stir powdered sugar and enough orange juice to a desired consistency. Drizzle over cooled cookies.

Makes 4 dozen.

WHITE CHOCOLATE CRANBERRY OATMEAL COOKIES

White chocolate chips may be used in place of chunks, if desired.

⅔ cup butter, softened
⅔ cup brown sugar, packed
2 eggs
1 teaspoon pure vanilla extract

1½ cups old-fashioned oats
1½ cups all-purpose flour
1 teaspoon baking soda
½ teaspoon salt
1 6-ounce package sweetened dried cranberries
⅔ cup white chocolate chunks

Preheat oven to 375°.
Beat butter and sugar until fluffy. Beat in eggs and vanilla extract.

In another bowl, mix oats, flour, soda and salt; add to creamed mixture; mix well. Stir in cranberries and chocolate.

Drop dough by rounded teaspoonfuls onto ungreased baking sheets. Bake 10–12 minutes or until golden brown. Cool on a wire rack.

Makes 2½ dozen.

Pies

APPLE-CRANBERRY FRIED PIES

Thawed frozen cranberries may be used if fresh are not available.

2 tart apples, such as Granny Smith, peeled, cored and chopped
1 cup fresh cranberries
½ cup granulated sugar
2 tablespoons honey
½ teaspoon ground cinnamon
⅛ teaspoon salt

1 teaspoon pure vanilla extract

1 15-ounce package refrigerated pie crusts
corn oil
1 tablespoon granulated sugar, mixed with ¼ teaspoon cinnamon

In a large saucepan, cook first six ingredients over medium heat 5 minutes; reduce heat to medium-low; cook, stirring occasionally until apples are tender, about 20 minutes. Stir in vanilla. Cool completely; drain; set aside.

Roll out pie crusts to 12-inch circles; cut each into 9 4-inch circles.

Spoon 1 level tablespoon fruit mixture onto half of each circle. Moisten edges with water, then fold dough over fruit mixture; press edges to seal, then crimp edges with a fork dipped in flour.

In a large heavy skillet, pour corn oil to a ½-inch depth. Heat the corn oil to 350°. Fry pies in batches, 1 minute on each side. Remove from skillet; sprinkle with sugar-cinnamon mixture.

Makes 1½ dozen.

APPLE-CRANBERRY-RASPBERRY PIE

Serve plain or with a dollop of whipped cream.

pastry for 9-inch two-crust pie

Filling
**2 cups chopped and peeled tart
  apples, such as Granny Smith**
2 cups whole cranberries, coarsely chopped
1 10-ounce package frozen dry-pack raspberries, thawed
1½ cups granulated sugar
3 tablespoons quick-cooking tapioca
½ teaspoon ground cinnamon
¼ teaspoon salt
½ teaspoon pure vanilla extract
¼ teaspoon almond extract

Glaze
**light cream or milk
granulated sugar**

Preheat oven to 375°.
Press bottom crust into a 9-inch pie plate, leaving an overhang.
Combine apples, cranberries and raspberries. In another bowl, mix remaining ingredients; add to fruit mixture, and toss to coat. Spoon mixture into pie crust. Fold edge under. Flute.

Roll top crust between lightly floured sheets of waxed paper. Trim dough to a circle 2½ inches smaller than upside-down pie plate. Cut a spiral strip starting from outside, about ¾ inch wide. Flip onto filling. Remove waxed paper. Separate strip gently with knife tip to form opened spiral. Brush spiral with light cream and sprinkle with sugar. Cover edge with aluminum foil to prevent burning.

Bake 25 minutes. Remove foil, and continue baking 25–35 minutes or until filling in center is bubbly. Cool to room temperature before serving. Refrigerate leftovers.

Makes 8 servings.

APPLE-CRANBERRY STREUSEL PIE

Serve warm with vanilla ice cream.

1 9-inch pastry shell

2 21-ounce cans apple pie filling
1 cup sweetened dried cranberries
½ teaspoon ground cinnamon
1 teaspoon pure vanilla extract

⅓ cup all-purpose flour
¼ cup brown sugar, packed
3 tablespoons butter

Preheat oven to 400°.
Bake pastry shell in a 9-inch pie plate, 8–10 minutes or until light brown; set aside.

Mix pie filling, cranberries, cinnamon and vanilla until well blended. Spoon mixture into baked shell.

Mix flour and brown sugar. Cut in butter with a pastry blender until coarse crumbs form; sprinkle evenly over filling.

Bake 35–45 minutes or until filling is bubbly. Remove from oven.

Makes 8 servings.

APPLESAUCE CRANBERRY CREAM CHEESE PIE

Serve plain or top with sweetened whipped cream.

1 9-inch graham cracker pie crust

Filling
1 8-ounce package cream cheese, softened
½ cup granulated sugar
1 cup applesauce
2 eggs, beaten
½ cup sweetened dried cranberries
2 tablespoons fresh lemon juice
1 teaspoon pure vanilla extract

Preheat oven to 350°.
Beat cream cheese until light. Beat in sugar until fluffy. Stir in remaining filling ingredients until well blended. Pour mixture into graham cracker crust. Bake about 55–65 minutes or until lightly browned. Remove from oven. Cool before serving. Store in refrigerator.

Makes 10 servings.

BRANDIED CRANBERRY PIE

Save this one for the party.

pastry for 9-inch two-crust pie

Filling
1 small seedless orange, finely chopped, including peel
2 tablespoons fresh lemon juice
1 21-ounce can peach pie filling
1 cup sweetened dried cranberries
½ cup dark raisins
½ cup granulated sugar
2 tablespoons minute-tapioca
⅓ cup brandy

Glaze
⅓ cup powdered sugar
1½ teaspoons pure vanilla extract or brandy
1½ tablespoons butter, softened

Preheat oven to 400°.
Line a 9-inch pie baking pan with bottom crust.

Filling: Mix all ingredients until well blended. Pour mixture into pie crust. Place top crust over filling. Seal and flute edges. Cut several slits in top crust. Cover edge of crust with baking foil to prevent over-browning.

Bake 40 minutes. Remove foil and continue baking 20 minutes. Cool completely on a wire rack. Drizzle with glaze. Refrigerate leftovers.

Glaze: Mix all ingredients until smooth.

Makes 8 servings.

CRAN-APPLE PIE

Serve warm with vanilla ice cream for a special treat.

pastry for 9-inch two-crust pie

Filling
4 cups apples, peeled, cored and sliced
1½ cups fresh or frozen whole cranberries
¼ cup raisins
1 cup granulated sugar
¼ cup brown sugar
¼ cup all-purpose flour
½ teaspoon ground cinnamon
¼ teaspoon salt
1 teaspoon pure vanilla extract

2 tablespoons butter, cut up

Preheat oven to 400°.
Combine all filling ingredients except butter; mix well. Pour into a pastry-lined pie plate. Dot with butter. Cover with top crust. Seal and flute edge; cut slits in top crust.

Bake 50–55 minutes or until apples are tender. Remove from oven; cool on a wire rack.

Makes 8 servings.

CRANBERRY CHEESECAKE PIE

Simple and delicious.

Crust
1¾ cups graham cracker crumbs
¼ cup granulated sugar
½ teaspoon ground cinnamon
⅛ teaspoon ground cloves
6 tablespoons butter, melted

Filling
12 ounces cream cheese, softened
½ cup granulated sugar
2 eggs
1 teaspoon pure vanilla extract
1 cup dairy sour cream

Topping
1 16-ounce can whole berry
 cranberry sauce
3 tablespoons granulated sugar
1 tablespoon cornstarch
2 tablespoons fresh orange juice
½ teaspoon pure vanilla extract
½ cup coarsely chopped walnuts

Preheat oven to 350°.
Crust: Mix all crust ingredients. Reserve ¼ cup. Press remaining crumbs onto bottom and up sides of a 9-inch pie plate. Bake 6 minutes. Cool; set aside.

Filling: Beat cream cheese until light. Add sugar and continue beating until fluffy. Beat in eggs, one at a time. Stir in remaining filling ingredients. Pour into prepared crust. Bake 40–45 minutes or until center is firm. Cool on rack to room temperature.

Topping: In a saucepan, mix all topping ingredients except vanilla, reserved crumbs and walnuts. Cook, stirring constantly, until thickened. Stir in vanilla. Cool. Spread over filling. Sprinkle with reserved crumbs and walnuts. Refrigerate; serve well-chilled. Refrigerate leftovers immediately.

Makes 8 servings.

FROZEN CRANBERRY CREAM CHEESE PIE

Perfect for a summer day.

1½ cups vanilla wafer crumbs
6 tablespoons butter, melted

2 3-ounce packages cream cheese, softened
1 14-ounce can sweetened condensed milk (not evaporated)
⅓ cup lemon juice
1 teaspoon pure vanilla extract
1 16-ounce can whole berry cranberry sauce, divided

sweetened whipped cream

Mix crumbs and butter in a bowl; press mixture onto bottom and up sides to rim of a 9-inch pie plate. Chill.

Beat cream cheese until fluffy. Gradually beat in condensed milk until smooth. Stir in lemon juice and vanilla. Reserve ½ cup cranberry sauce. Add remaining sauce to cheese mixture. Pour into prepared crust.

Cover and freeze until firm, about 6 hours. Garnish with whipped cream and reserved cranberry sauce. Freeze leftovers.

Makes 8 servings.

NO-BAKE CRANBERRY CREAM PIE

Also good in a graham cracker crust.

1 9-inch baked pastry shell

¾ cup granulated sugar
2 teaspoons cornstarch
¼ cup cold water
2 cups whole cranberries

6 ounces cream cheese, softened
1 cup powdered sugar
1 teaspoon pure vanilla extract
1 cup whipping cream, whipped

In a saucepan, mix granulated sugar, cornstarch and water until smooth.
Add cranberries. Bring to a boil, stirring constantly for about 2 minutes.
Reduce heat; cook, stirring occasionally, until cranberries pop, about
5 minutes. Remove from heat; cool.

Beat cream cheese, powdered sugar and vanilla until fluffy. Fold in whipped
cream. Spread evenly into baked pastry shell. Top with cooled cranberry
mixture. Chill well. Store in refrigerator.

Makes 8 servings.

PEAR-CRANBERRY PIE

Serve warm or at room temperature.

pastry for 9-inch two-crust pie

1 cup granulated sugar
3 tablespoons quick-cooking tapioca
5 cups thinly sliced, peeled and cored pears
1½ cups fresh cranberries
1 teaspoon pure vanilla extract

1 tablespoon milk
coarse sugar

Preheat oven to 375°.
Line a 9-inch pie plate with bottom crust.

In a large saucepan, mix granulated sugar and tapioca. Stir in pears and cranberries until coated; let stand 15 minutes or until syrup begins to form, stirring occasionally. Bring mixture to a boil, then reduce heat. Cover and simmer 3–5 minutes or until pears are just softened and cranberries begin to pop. Stir in vanilla. Pour mixture into prepared pie plate. Trim crust to edge of pie plate. Cover with top crust. Seal and crimp edges; cut several slits on top crust. Brush with milk; sprinkle with coarse sugar.

Cover edge of pie with baking foil to prevent over-browning; bake 25 minutes. Remove foil and bake 30–35 minutes or until top is golden. Remove from oven; cool on a wire rack. Refrigerate leftovers.

Makes 8 servings.

WHITE CHOCOLATE CRANBERRY PECAN PIE

Serve plain or garnish with sweetened whipped cream.

pastry for 9-inch crust

1½ cups fresh or frozen whole cranberries
1 cup pecan halves
1 cup white chocolate chips (the kind with butter
   listed in ingredients)

3 eggs
¾ cup brown sugar, packed
¾ cup light corn syrup
3 tablespoons all-purpose flour
1 teaspoon pure vanilla extract
1 teaspoon grated fresh orange peel (optional)

Preheat oven to 400°.
Line a 9-inch pie plate with unbaked crust; layer with cranberries, pecans and
white chocolate chips.

In a large bowl, beat eggs. Stir in brown sugar, syrup, flour, vanilla and
orange peel (if desired) until well blended. Pour over cranberry mixture.

Bake 40–50 minutes or until crust is golden brown and filling is set in center;
cover with baking foil the last 15 minutes of baking. Cool on a wire rack
2 hours before serving. Store in refrigerator.

Makes 8 servings.

Desserts

APPLE-CRANBERRY BAKE

Simple and delicious…serve with sweetened whipped cream.

4 cups chopped, peeled apples
2 cups fresh or frozen cranberries
1 cup water

1¼ cups granulated sugar
1 teaspoon pure vanilla extract
½ cup chopped walnuts
2 tablespoons cornstarch
¼ teaspoon salt
¼ teaspoon ground cinnamon

Topping
1 12-ounce can refrigerated
    biscuits
¼ cup granulated sugar
½ teaspoon ground cinnamon
3 tablespoons butter, melted
¼ cup chopped walnuts

Preheat oven to 400°.
In a large saucepan, cook apples, cranberries and water over medium heat
5 minutes.

In a small bowl, mix 1¼ cups sugar, vanilla, ½ cup walnuts, cornstarch, salt
and ¼ teaspoon cinnamon; stir into apple mixture, and cook until thickened,
about 4 minutes. Pour mixture into an ungreased 13x9-inch baking pan.

Topping: Separate dough into 10 biscuits; separate each biscuit into 2 layers.
In a small bowl, mix sugar and cinnamon. Dip one side of each biscuit in
melted butter, then in sugar mixture. Place biscuits, sugared side up, over
hot apple mixture, overlapping to make 2 rows. Sprinkle with walnuts.

Bake 20–25 minutes or until deep golden brown. Serve warm.
Refrigerate leftovers.

Makes 10 servings.

APPLE-CRANBERRY-PEAR BAKED COMPOTE

Serve this tasty compote with vanilla ice cream.

1½ cups fresh cranberries
½ cup sweet red wine
½ cup apple cider
5 tablespoons granulated sugar
1 1-inch strip fresh lemon rind

½ cup applesauce

4 cups Golden Delicious apples, peeled and sliced
2 cups pears, cored and cut into ¼-inch wedges

Preheat oven to 400°.
In a saucepan, mix first five ingredients; bring to a simmer over medium heat, stirring occasionally. Remove from heat; stir in applesauce.

Mix apples and pears in a buttered 11x7-inch baking dish. Pour cranberry mixture on top. Cover and bake 25 minutes. Uncover and bake 10 minutes or until fruit is tender, basting occasionally with liquid from dish. Remove rind. Serve warm. Refrigerate leftovers.

Makes 6 servings.

CRANBERRY BREAD PUDDING

Bread pudding with a little tang.

16 slices firm-textured white
   bread, cubed
1 cup dried cranberries
¼ cup golden raisins

2 12-ounce cans evaporated milk
4 large eggs, slightly beaten
4 tablespoons butter, melted
¾ cup brown sugar, packed
1 tablespoon pure vanilla extract
1 teaspoon ground cinnamon
½ teaspoon ground nutmeg

Vanilla sauce
1 cup granulated sugar
1 tablespoon all-purpose flour
⅓ cup butter
1 cup light cream
½ teaspoon pure vanilla extract

Preheat oven to 350°.
Grease a 12x8-inch baking dish.

Mix bread cubes, cranberries and raisins. In another bowl, mix remaining pudding ingredients and pour over bread mixture; mix well. Pour into prepared baking dish. Let stand 10 minutes. Bake 35–45 minutes or until a knife inserted in center comes out clean.

Vanilla sauce: In a saucepan, stir together sugar and flour; stir in butter and cream. Cook over medium heat, stirring constantly, until thick. Remove from heat; stir in vanilla extract.

Serve pudding warm with vanilla sauce. Refrigerate leftovers.

Makes 8 servings.

CRANBERRY CRÈME BRÛLÉE

If you use a torch to carmelize sugar, use raw sugar in place of superfine sugar.

16 tablespoons cranberry sauce
1 cup half & half
1 vanilla bean
½ teaspoon pure vanilla extract

1 egg
8 egg yolks
⅔ cup granulated sugar
1½ cups heavy cream, cold
2 tablespoons superfine sugar

Preheat oven to 325°.
Spoon 2 tablespoons cranberry sauce into each of 8 4-ounce ungreased ramekins. In a small saucepan stir half & half, vanilla bean and vanilla extract over medium heat just until scalded; do not boil. Discard vanilla bean.

Fill a large bowl with water and ice; set aside. In another bowl, mix egg, yolks and granulated sugar until blended. Gradually stir in the scalded half & half mixture. Place bowl into the ice bowl; cool completely. Stir heavy cream into cooled mixture.

Spoon equal amounts over cranberry sauce in ramekins. Place ramekins in a large baking pan; add hot water in baking pan to come halfway up the sides of ramekins. Cover baking pan tightly with foil. Bake until custard is set but still shakes a little in the center, about 35 minutes. Remove ramekins from water; refrigerate and cool completely.

Preheat broiler. Sprinkle top of each custard with superfine sugar; spread evenly, tapping out any excess. Place ramekins on a baking sheet, and broil until top is melted and caramelized, about 30 seconds. Serve while sugar is warm. Refrigerate leftovers.

Makes 8 servings.

CREAMY CRANBERRY RICE PUDDING

Cranberries and raisins in a creamy pudding.

1⅓ cups water
⅔ cup long-grain white rice (not instant)
1 12-ounce can evaporated milk
½ cup sweetened dried cranberries
½ cup raisins
½ cup granulated sugar
1½ teaspoons pure vanilla extract
¼ teaspoon ground nutmeg
¼ teaspoon salt

2 large eggs, lightly beaten in a bowl
ground cinnamon

Bring water and rice to a boil in a small saucepan. Reduce heat to low; cover and cook until liquid is absorbed, about 15 minutes. Stir in evaporated milk, cranberries, raisins, sugar, vanilla, nutmeg and salt. Bring to a boil.

Stir a portion of rice mixture into the eggs, then stir back into rice mixture. Mix well with wire whisk. Bring to a boil. Cook, stirring constantly, 2 minutes. Sprinkle with a little ground cinnamon when serving. Serve warm or chilled. Refrigerate leftovers.

Makes 6 servings.

CHOCOLATE CRANBERRY-SAUCED POACHED PEARS

An elegant dessert.

6 cups cranberry juice cocktail
1 cup granulated sugar
6 Bartlett pears, peeled, cored with stems intact*
1 16-ounce can jellied cranberry sauce
½ cup chocolate chips

Stir juice and sugar in a large saucepan; bring to a boil over high heat. Place pears in pan, cover and reduce heat. Simmer over low heat about 15 minutes or until pears are tender when pierced with a fork, turning pears several times during cooking. Remove from heat; let cool in liquid at room temperature.

In a medium saucepan, stir cranberry sauce and chocolate chips over medium heat, whisking until smooth.

Remove pears from liquid; drain well. To serve, spoon ¼ cup chocolate cranberry sauce on each dessert plate. Place a pear on each plate. Spoon remaining sauce over tops of pears. Refrigerate leftovers.

Makes 6 servings.

*Peel the pears, then core from the bottom using a small paring knife. Core far enough into the round part of the pear to get to the seeds. Scoop the seeds out using a small melon baller or small teaspoon.

CRANBERRY FOOL

Fool is a British dessert made of fruit and cream.

1 16-ounce can jellied cranberry sauce
1 tablespoon grated fresh orange peel
1 teaspoon almond extract
1 cup heavy cream, whipped

Mix cranberry sauce, orange peel and almond extract. Fold in whipped cream. Spoon into dessert glasses. Chill until set. Garnish with additional whipped cream and an orange slice.

Makes 6 servings.

CRANBERRY ICE CREAM

A tasty treat.

1 12-ounce package fresh cranberries
¼ cup water
2¾ cups whipping cream
1 cup granulated sugar
1 teaspoon pure vanilla extract

Rinse cranberries; place in a nonreactive saucepan with water. Cook covered, stirring occasionally, about 10 minutes or until cranberries are soft. Purée through a food mill and strain. Measure 1¼ cups.

In another saucepan, warm cream and sugar, stirring until sugar has dissolved. Whisk the cranberry purée into the cream mixture. Stir in vanilla. Chill. Freeze in an ice cream maker according to manufacturer's directions. Freeze leftovers.

Makes about 1 quart.

CRANBERRY SORBET

A refreshing dessert.

2 cups cranberries
¼ cup orange juice
1 tablespoon grated orange zest
3 cups water, divided
1 cup granulated sugar
1 tablespoon lemon juice

In a saucepan, cook cranberries, orange juice, orange zest, and ½ cup water over medium heat until cranberries pop, about 7 minutes. Coarsely mash cranberries. Add sugar, lemon juice and remaining water. Simmer, stirring often, until a syrup forms. Remove from heat; let cool. Refrigerate several hours. Freeze in an ice cream maker according to manufacturer's directions. Freeze leftovers.

Makes 1 quart.

CREAMY CRANBERRY-ORANGE GELATIN DESSERT

Sweet, tangy and creamy.

1½ cups boiling water
1 package (8-serving size) cranberry flavor gelatin
1 16-ounce can whole berry cranberry sauce
1½ cups cold water
1 15-ounce can Mandarin oranges, drained, cut up

1½ cups graham cracker crumbs
½ cup granulated sugar, divided
½ cup butter, melted

1 8-ounce package cream cheese, softened
2 tablespoons milk
2 8-ounce containers non-dairy whipped topping, thawed

In a large bowl, stir boiling water and gelatin until completely dissolved. Stir in cranberry sauce until melted. Stir in cold water. Refrigerate until slightly thickened but not set. Stir in Mandarin oranges.

In a 13x9-inch glass baking dish, stir graham cracker crumbs, ¼ cup sugar and butter until blended. Press firmly onto bottom of dish. Chill.

Beat cream cheese, remaining ¼ cup sugar and milk with wire whisk until smooth. Gently stir in 1 container thawed whipped topping. Spread evenly over crumb crust. Spoon gelatin mixture over cream cheese layer. Refrigerate until firm. When serving, top with remaining thawed whipped topping. Store in refrigerator.

Makes 12 servings.

ORANGE-CRANBERRY TRIFLE

A tasty dessert.

1 8-ounce package cream cheese, softened
½ cup granulated sugar
1 teaspoon ground cinnamon
1 teaspoon pure orange extract, divided
2 cups thawed non-dairy whipped topping
1 cup whole berry cranberry sauce

1 10-ounce loaf pound cake, thinly sliced
½ cup milk
1 teaspoon pure vanilla extract

¼ cup toasted sliced almonds

Beat cream cheese, sugar, cinnamon and ½ teaspoon orange extract until smooth. Gently stir in whipped topping and cranberry sauce; set aside.

Arrange one-third of the cake slices on bottom of an 8-inch square baking dish. Mix milk, vanilla and ½ teaspoon orange extract; drizzle approximately 2 tablespoons of milk mixture over cake slices, then spread one-third of cream cheese mixture over cake slices. Repeat for second and third layers. Sprinkle top with sliced almonds. Cover and refrigerate until well chilled before serving. Store in refrigerator.

Makes 8 servings.

STEAMED PEAR-CRANBERRY PUDDING

Two cups coarsely chopped fresh cranberries can be used instead of the pears and cranberries. Use the same cooking instructions.

1½ cups all-purpose flour
2 teaspoons baking soda
½ teaspoon salt

½ cup hot water
½ cup molasses
1 teaspoon pure vanilla extract

1–2 ripe Anjou pears, cored
　and diced to equal 1 cup
1 cup halved fresh cranberries

Butter sauce
6 tablespoons butter
¾ cup granulated sugar
6 tablespoons half & half
½ teaspoon pure vanilla extract

Sift flour, soda and salt, add pears and cranberries; mix well. Combine hot water, molasses and vanilla extract; stir into dry ingredients.

Pour mixture into a greased 1½-quart metal mold; fill only ⅔ full to allow for expansion during cooking. Cover with lid or greased cooking foil. Place on a rack in a deep kettle, adding boiling water to come halfway up side of mold. Do not submerge mold. Cover kettle and simmer 2 hours or until a wooden pick inserted center comes out clean.

Cool mold on a wire rack 10 minutes. Loosen pudding and invert onto a serving plate.

Butter sauce: Combine first three ingredients in a saucepan, cook and stir constantly until sugar is dissolved. Stir in vanilla extract.

Serve warm or cold with butter sauce. Refrigerate leftovers.

Makes 6 servings.

Tarts
Tortes

APPLE-CRANBERRY TART

Top with vanilla ice cream.

1 crust from a 15-ounce package refrigerated unbaked pie crust

1 21-ounce can apple pie filling
1 cup fresh or frozen whole cranberries, chopped
¼ cup chopped walnuts
1 teaspoon ground cinnamon
½ teaspoon pure vanilla extract

1 teaspoon granulated sugar

Preheat oven to 400°.
Unwrap the pie crust; press seams together firmly, and place into a 9-inch pie plate.

Combine all ingredients except sugar; mix well. Spoon mixture into prepared crust. Fold edges of pastry over fruit mixture, pleating so crust lies flat (most of the fruit mixture will be covered). Sprinkle sugar over crust. Bake 15 minutes, then reduce heat to 350° and bake about 45 minutes or until fruit is bubbly and crust is golden brown. Serve warm. Refrigerate leftovers.

Makes 8 servings.

APRICOT-CRANBERRY TART

Garnish with whipped cream when serving.

1 15-ounce package refrigerated
  unbaked pie crust (2 crusts)

½ cup granulated sugar
3 tablespoons cornstarch
1 teaspoon ground cinnamon
½ teaspoon ground ginger
½ teaspoon ground nutmeg
¼ teaspoon salt

3 15-ounce cans apricot halves,
  drained and cut up
½ cup dried cranberries

1 egg white, mixed with
  1 tablespoon milk
1 tablespoon granulated sugar

Preheat oven to 450°.
Line a 9-inch tart pan that has a removable bottom with one pie crust.
Press into fluted sides of pan; trim edges. Line with a double thickness of
baking foil. Bake 8 minutes; remove foil, and bake 4 minutes or until set
and dry. Remove from oven. Reduce heat to 375°.

Mix ½ cup sugar, cornstarch, cinnamon, ginger, nutmeg and salt. Stir in
apricots and cranberries. Spoon into prepared crust.

Place remaining crust on a floured surface; use small cookie cutter to cut
20 small star or other shapes. Brush shapes with egg mixture and sprinkle
equally with 1 tablespoon sugar; place pastry shapes on filling. Bake
35–40 minutes or until filling is bubbly. Cool on a wire rack. Remove side
of pan and place tart on a serving plate. Refrigerate leftovers.

Makes 8 servings.

CRANBERRY CREAM TART

Very tasty and simple to prepare.

Crust
**1¼ cups graham
   cracker crumbs**
2 tablespoons granulated sugar
⅓ cup chopped pecans, toasted
6 tablespoons butter

Filling
1 8-ounce package cream cheese, softened
⅓ cup powdered sugar
1 teaspoon pure vanilla extract
2 tablespoons fresh orange juice
1 cup whipping cream

Topping
1 cup granulated sugar
2½ cups fresh cranberries
1 tablespoon water
**2½ tablespoons cornstarch
   dissolved in 2 tablespoons
   water**

Preheat oven to 350°.
Crust: Combine all ingredients. Press mixture onto bottom and sides of an 11-inch tart pan. Bake until lightly browned, 8–10 minutes. Cool completely.

Filling: Beat cream cheese and sugar until light and fluffy. Beat in vanilla and orange juice. Beat whipping cream to soft peaks; fold into cream cheese mixture, then spoon into prepared cooled crust.

Topping: Bring sugar, cranberries and water to a boil, stirring constantly until cranberries pop. Quickly stir in cornstarch mixture and continue cooking, stirring until thickened. Remove from heat; cool. Spread over filling. Cover with plastic food wrap and chill before serving. Store in refrigerator.

Makes 8 servings.

CREAM CHEESE CRANBERRY TARTLETS

Garnish with whipped cream and sweetened dried cranberries.

Crust
1¼ cups all-purpose flour
½ cup ground toasted
  walnuts
¼ cup granulated sugar
½ cup cold butter
  (no substitution)
2 beaten egg yolks mixed
  with 2 tablespoons cold water

Filling
1 8-ounce package cream cheese,
  softened
½ cup granulated sugar
2 teaspoons all-purpose flour
1 egg
¼ cup sweetened dried cranberries
1 teaspoon finely shredded fresh
  orange peel
1 tablespoon fresh orange juice
1 teaspoon pure vanilla extract

Preheat oven to 375°.
Crust: Stir flour, ground walnuts and sugar together. Cut in butter with a pastry blender to form pea-size crumbs. Gradually stir egg mixture into flour mixture. Gently knead dough just to form a ball. Cover with plastic wrap; chill for easy handling. Flatten ball on a lightly floured surface. Roll dough from center to edges to ⅛-inch thickness. Cut dough into ten 4½-inch circles. Line 3-inch fluted tartlet pans with circles of dough; trim to edges of pans. Prick bottom of dough with a fork. Place pans on a cookie sheet. Bake for 8–12 minutes.

Filling: Beat cream cheese, sugar and flour until combined. Beat in egg. Stir in remaining filling ingredients. Spoon into baked tartlet shells. Bake about 15 minutes or until center is almost set. Remove tartlet pans from cookie sheet. Cool on a wire rack 15 minutes; remove tartlets from pans; cool on a rack.Refrigerate and chill well before serving. Refrigerate leftovers.

Makes 10 servings.

CHOCOLATE CRANBERRY TORTE

A nice dessert for the holidays.

Sauce
- **1 cup fresh cranberries**
- **¾ cup water**
- **⅓ cup granulated sugar**
- **2 tablespoons black raspberry liqueur**

Glaze
- **1 cup whipping cream**
- **10 oz. bittersweet chocolate, chopped**
- **¾ cup black raspberry liqueur**

Torte
- **1 cup sweetened dried cranberries, divided**
- **⅓ cup raspberry liqueur**
- **1 cup butter, cut up**
- **12 oz. bittersweet chocolate, chopped**
- **1½ cups granulated sugar**
- **6 large eggs**
- **⅔ cup all-purpose flour**
- **½ teaspoon salt**

Sauce: Bring first three ingredients to a boil over high heat, stirring until sugar dissolves. Reduce heat; cook until cranberries pop. Purée mixture in food processor. Strain purée into a bowl; discard seeds. Stir in liqueur. Cover and chill 2 hours.

Torte: Preheat oven to 350°. Butter and flour a 9-inch springform pan. Line bottom with parchment paper. Stir ¾ cup cranberries and liqueur in a saucepan until liqueur simmers. Cool; drain and reserve cranberries and liqueur separately. Melt butter in saucepan; remove from heat. Add chocolate and let stand 1 minute; whisk until melted and smooth. Whisk in sugar, then eggs, 1 at a time. Whisk in reserved liqueur. Stir in flour and salt until blended. Stir in reserved cranberries. Spoon into prepared pan. Bake until top is puffed and cracked and wooden pick inserted in center comes out clean, about 1 hour. Cool in pan on cake rack.

Glaze: Simmer cream. Remove from heat and add chocolate; whisk until melted and smooth. Stir in liqueur. Let stand until thickened slightly, whisking occasionally, about 2 hours.

Place torte and cake rack on a baking sheet. Loosen torte and remove pan sides. Place an 8-inch cardboard round on torte, turn torte over onto cake rack. Remove pan bottom, peel off paper. Smooth 1½ cups glaze over top and sides. Freeze until set. Smooth remaining glaze over torte. Sprinkle with ¼ cup cranberries; freeze until glaze is firm, about 15 minutes. Refrigerate. Serve at room temperature.

Makes 8 servings.

CRANBERRY LINZER TORTE

Garnish with whipped cream when serving.

Crust
1 cup almonds
1½ cups all-purpose flour
1 cup butter
1 cup granulated sugar
2 large egg yolks
1 tablespoon grated orange peel
1 tablespoon unsweetened cocoa powder
2 teaspoons ground cinnamon
½ teaspoon ground cloves

Filling
1 12-ounce package fresh or
  thawed frozen cranberries
  (3 cups)
1 cup granulated sugar
1 tablespoon grated orange peel

Crust: Process almonds in food processor until finely ground. Add remaining ingredients; whirl until dough holds together. Form dough into a firm ball; remove ½ cup dough and set aside. Press remaining dough evenly over bottom and 1½ inches up sides of a greased 9-inch cake pan with removable rim. Set aside.

Preheat oven to 350°.
Filling: Bring all filling ingredients to a boil over high heat in a 2½-quart saucepan, stirring often, until mixture has a soft jam consistency. Remove from heat; let cool 15 minutes, stirring occasionally. Pour cooled mixture into prepared crust. Break the reserved crust dough into pea-size lumps, and sprinkle evenly over filling. Bake until crust is browned at edges, about 1 hour. Cool before serving. Refrigerate leftovers.

Makes 12 servings.

CRANBERRY TORTE

Use other flavor of gelatin if desired.

3 egg yolks
½ cup granulated sugar
1 cup graham cracker crumbs
1½ teaspoons pure
    vanilla extract

3 egg whites
½ cup granulated sugar
½ cup chopped nuts

1 16-ounce can whole
    cranberry sauce
½ cup brown sugar
1 3-ounce package
    orange flavor gelatin
2 cups whipped cream

Preheat oven to 350°.
Beat egg yolks and gradually beat in ½ cup granulated sugar until thick and lemon colored. Stir in graham cracker crumbs and vanilla extract.

In another bowl, beat egg whites until fluffy. Beat in ½ cup granulated sugar until shiny and stiff peaks form. Fold in egg yolk mixture and chopped nuts. Spoon batter into 2 greased 8-inch pie plates. Bake 30 minutes. Remove from oven to a wire rack. Cool.

In a saucepan, mix cranberry sauce and brown sugar; bring to a boil over medium heat, stirring constantly. Remove from heat. Stir in dry orange gelatin until dissolved. Cool completely. Spread half the cranberry sauce on one cooled graham cracker shell. Top with half the whipped cream. Place second cooled graham cracker shell on top and repeat layering with remaining cranberry sauce and whipped cream. Store in refrigerator.

Makes 6 servings.

CREAMY CRANBERRY TORTE

Simple and delicious.

1 8-ounce package cream cheese, softened
¼ cup granulated sugar
½ cup whipping cream, whipped with 1 tablespoon
  powdered sugar and ½ teaspoon pure vanilla extract

1 10-ounce frozen pound cake, thawed
1 14-ounce jar cranberry-orange sauce

Beat cream cheese with sugar until fluffy. Fold in whipped cream.

Split cake horizontally into 4 layers. Spread bottom layer with ½ cup cranberry-orange sauce; top with second cake layer. Spread second layer with ⅔ cup cream cheese mixture; top with third cake layer. Spread third layer with ½ cup cranberry-orange sauce. Cover with top cake layer. Frost top and sides of torte with remaining cream cheese mixture. Chill well before serving. Refrigerate leftovers.

Makes 8 servings.

Muffins
Breads
Scones
Biscuits

BLUEBERRY-CRANBERRY MUFFINS

Blueberries and cranberries...a good muffin combination.

2 cups all-purpose flour
½ cup granulated sugar
2 teaspoons baking powder
½ teaspoon salt

1 egg, beaten
1 cup whole milk
⅓ cup margarine, melted
1 teaspoon pure vanilla extract

¾ cup fresh or frozen blueberries
½ cup sweetened dried cranberries
2 teaspoons granulated sugar

Preheat oven to 400°.
Grease or paper line muffin pan.

Mix first four ingredients until well blended. Add next four ingredients, stir only until moistened.

Stir in blueberries and cranberries just until incorporated.

Spoon batter into prepared pan; sprinkle tops equally with 2 teaspoons sugar. Bake 20–25 minutes. Remove from pan. Serve immediately or cool on a rack.

Makes 12 muffins.

CAPPUCCINO CRANBERRY MUFFINS

A nice midmorning treat.

Dry ingredients
1¾ cups all-purpose flour
⅔ cup granulated sugar
1½ teaspoons baking powder
½ teaspoon baking soda
3 tablespoons unsweetened cocoa powder
1 tablespoon instant coffee powder
½ teaspoon ground cinnamon
½ teaspoon salt

Wet ingredients
¾ cup whole milk
1 egg, beaten
6 tablespoons corn oil
1 6-ounce package sweetened dried cranberries

Preheat oven to 375°.
Grease or paper line muffin pan.

Combine all dry ingredients; mix well.

In another bowl, combine all wet ingredients; mix well.

Combine wet and dry mixtures in large bowl. Stir only to moisten. Spoon batter into prepared pan. Bake 20–25 minutes or until a wooden pick inserted in center comes out clean. Remove from pan to a cooling rack.

Makes 12 muffins.

FRESH CRANBERRY MUFFINS

Fresh cranberries and orange in this good muffin.

2 cups all-purpose flour
1 cup granulated sugar
1½ teaspoons baking powder
½ teaspoon baking soda

¼ cup butter or margarine, melted and cooled
1 egg, beaten
1 teaspoon pure vanilla extract
1 teaspoon grated fresh orange peel
¾ cup fresh orange juice

1½ cups fresh cranberries, coarsely chopped

Preheat oven to 375°.
Grease or paper line muffin pan.

Mix first four ingredients until well blended.

In another bowl, mix next five ingredients; stir mixture into flour mixture only to moisten. Stir in cranberries. Spoon batter into prepared pan. Bake 20–25 minutes or until golden brown. Remove from pan to a wire rack.

Makes 15 muffins.

LOLA'S CRANBERRY-APPLE MUFFINS

A favorite muffin for Christmas breakfast.

Dry ingredients
1½ cup all-purpose flour
½ cup granulated sugar
1 teaspoon ground cinnamon
½ teaspoon baking soda
¼ teaspoon baking powder
¼ teaspoon salt

Wet ingredients
1 egg, slightly beaten
1 cup peeled shredded apple
⅓ cup milk
⅓ cup corn oil
1 teaspoon pure vanilla extract

Filling
½ cup cranberry sauce,
mixed with ½ teaspoon
shredded orange peel

Glaze
½ cup powdered sugar,
mixed with 2 to 3 teaspoons
orange juice

Preheat oven to 375°.
Grease or paper line muffin pan.

Mix all dry ingredients. Add wet ingredients. Stir just until moistened. Fill greased 2½-inch muffin baking tins half full. Make a well in center of each, and spoon 2 teaspoons cranberry filling into each.

Bake 18–25 minutes. Remove from pan. Drizzle with glaze while warm. Refrigerate leftovers.

Makes 12 muffins.

ORANGE-CRANBERRY OAT BRAN MUFFINS

Cholesterol free…from my book *The Muffins are Coming*.

Dry ingredients
1¾ cups all-purpose flour
¾ cup oat bran
2 teaspoons baking powder
½ teaspoon salt
½ cup granulated sugar
1 tablespoon nonfat dry milk

Wet ingredients
¼ cup margarine, melted
¾ cup fresh orange juice
2 egg whites, beaten
1 teaspoon pure vanilla extract
1 tablespoon grated orange rind
1 cup fresh cranberries, halved

Preheat oven to 400°.
Grease or paper line muffin pan.

Combine all dry ingredients; mix well.

In another bowl, combine all wet ingredients; mix well.

Combine dry and wet ingredients. Stir only to moisten; batter will be lumpy.
Spoon into prepared pan. Bake 20–25 minutes. Remove from pan; cool on
a rack. Serve warm with marmalade.

Makes 12 muffins.

CRANBERRY CORN MUFFINS

To freeze and save for another day, cool muffins and place in a plastic food bag; freeze.

1 cup all-purpose flour
¾ cup cornmeal
⅓ cup granulated sugar
2 teaspoons baking powder
¼ teaspoon salt

1 egg, beaten
¾ cup buttermilk
¼ cup corn oil
½ cup finely shredded lemon peel

1 cup coarsely chopped fresh cranberries, mixed
  with 2 tablespoons granulated sugar
¼ cup finely chopped walnuts

Preheat oven to 400°.
Grease or paper line twelve 2½-inch muffin cups.

Mix first five ingredients. In another bowl, mix egg, buttermilk, corn oil and lemon peel; stir into first mixture until just moistened, batter will be lumpy. Stir in cranberry-sugar mixture and walnuts. Fill each prepared cup ⅔ full with batter.

Bake 20–25 minutes. Remove from cups to a rack. Serve warm.

Makes 12 muffins.

BANANA-CRANBERRY BREAD

A little tang added to banana bread.

1 cup granulated sugar
½ cup butter or margarine, softened
1 cup mashed ripe banana
¼ cup milk
2 eggs
1 teaspoon pure vanilla extract

2 cups all-purpose flour
2 teaspoons baking powder
¼ teaspoon baking soda
½ cup coarsely chopped walnuts
1 6-ounce package sweetened dried cranberries

Preheat oven to 350°.
Grease an 8½x4½x2½-inch loaf pan.

Beat sugar and butter until blended. Add banana, milk, eggs and vanilla.

In another bowl, mix flour, baking powder and baking soda; stir into sugar mixture until just moistened. Stir in walnuts and cranberries. Spoon batter evenly into prepared pan.

Bake about 1 hour or until a wooden pick inserted comes out clean. Remove from pan. Cool completely on a rack. Refrigerate leftovers.

Makes 1 loaf.

CHOCOLATE CRANBERRY BREAD

Offer this bread with softened cream cheese.

1½ cups all-purpose flour
1 teaspoon baking powder
½ teaspoon baking soda
½ teaspoon salt
¾ cup dairy sour cream
¾ cup unsweetened cocoa powder

6 tablespoons butter, softened
1 cup granulated sugar
2 large eggs
1 teaspoon pure vanilla extract
1 cup fresh or frozen cranberries, coarsely chopped
2 bars (1.5-ounce each) solid dark chocolate, coarsely chopped

Preheat oven to 350°.
Grease a 9x5x3-inch loaf pan.
Mix flour, baking powder, baking soda and salt; set aside. In another bowl, blend sour cream and cocoa powder; set aside.

In a third bowl, beat butter until creamy. Gradually beat in sugar until fluffy. Beat in eggs, one at a time. Beat in vanilla. Stir in flour mixture alternately with sour cream mixture, just until combined. Stir in cranberries and chopped dark chocolate. Spoon batter into prepared pan.

Bake 55–65 minutes or until a wooden pick inserted center comes out clean. Cool in pan on a wire rack 15 minutes. Remove from pan; cool completely on a wire rack. Refrigerate leftovers.

Makes 1 loaf.

CRANBERRY NUT BREAD

A flavorful cranberry bread.

2 cups all-purpose flour
1 cup granulated sugar
1½ teaspoons baking powder
½ teaspoon baking soda
1 teaspoon salt
6 tablespoons butter, cut up

1 teaspoon freshly grated orange zest
¾ cup fresh orange juice
1 teaspoon pure vanilla extract
2 large eggs
1¼ cups coarsely chopped cranberries
¾ cup coarsely chopped walnuts

Preheat oven to 350°.
Generously grease a 9x5x3-inch loaf pan.

Blend flour, sugar, baking powder, baking soda and salt. Add butter; blend until mixture resembles coarse meal. Place mixture in a large bowl.

In a small bowl, whisk together orange zest, juice, vanilla and eggs. Stir into flour mixture until batter is just combined. Stir in cranberries and walnuts. Spoon batter into prepared pan.

Bake about 1 hour and 25 minutes or until a wooden pick inserted in center comes out clean. Remove from oven; cool in pan 15 minutes. Remove from pan; cool on a rack. Refrigerate leftovers.

Makes 1 loaf.

MARY DOW'S CRANBERRY-SWEET POTATO BREAD

A good breakfast treat…serve warm with softened butter.

1 8-ounce package cream cheese, softened
1 cup granulated sugar
1 cup peeled and mashed fresh baked sweet potatoes
2 large eggs
1 teaspoon pure vanilla extract
1 teaspoon ground cinnamon
½ teaspoon ground nutmeg
1½ cups all-purpose baking mix
1 cup sweetened dried cranberries

Preheat oven to 350°.
Grease a 9x5x3-inch loaf pan.

Beat cream cheese and sugar until light. Beat in sweet potatoes, eggs, vanilla, cinnamon and nutmeg. Stir in baking mix and cranberries until just blended, do not over-mix. Spoon mixture into prepared pan.

Bake 45–60 minutes or until a wooden pick inserted in center comes out clean. Remove from oven; cool in pan 15 minutes. Remove from pan. When completely cool, wrap in plastic food wrap. Refrigerate leftovers.

Makes 1 loaf.

PUMPKIN-CRANBERRY BREAD

Serve this delicious bread plain or with softened butter.

2 cups all-purpose flour
2 teaspoons pumpkin pie spice
1 teaspoon baking powder
¾ teaspoon salt
½ teaspoon baking soda

6 tablespoons butter, softened
1 cup granulated sugar
2 large eggs

1 cup canned pure pumpkin
(not pie filling)
1 teaspoon pure vanilla extract

⅔ cup buttermilk
½ cup sweetened dried cranberries
½ cup coarsely chopped walnuts

1 tablespoon granulated sugar

Preheat oven to 350°.
Grease a 9x5x3-inch loaf pan.

Mix together first five dry ingredients; set aside.

Beat butter until fluffy. Gradually beat in 1 cup sugar. Beat in eggs, one at a time. Beat in pumpkin and vanilla. Beat in dry ingredients alternately with buttermilk in two additions. Fold in cranberries and walnuts. Spoon batter into prepared pan. Sprinkle with 1 tablespoon granulated sugar.

Bake about 1 hour and 10 minutes or until a wooden pick inserted in center comes out clean. Remove from oven; cool in pan 15 minutes. Remove from pan to a wire rack; cool completely. Serve or wrap in food plastic wrap and refrigerate.

Makes 1 loaf.

RAISIN CRANBERRY BREAD

A good treat to add to the Thanksgiving feast!

2⅔ cups all-purpose flour
1 tablespoon baking powder
1 teaspoon baking soda
1 teaspoon salt
¼ teaspoon pumpkin pie spice

½ cup margarine
½ cup brown sugar

½ cup orange marmalade
¾ cup reduced-fat small curd
   cottage cheese
2 eggs, slightly beaten
½ teaspoon pure vanilla extract
Grated rind of 1 lemon
Grated rind of 1 orange
¼ cup fresh orange juice

½ cup golden raisins
1 cup cranberries, coarsely
   chopped

Preheat oven to 325°.
Coat a 9x5x3-inch loaf pan with nonstick cooking spray.

Mix together first five ingredients; set aside.

In another bowl, beat margarine and brown sugar until creamy. Add
next seven ingredients; mix thoroughly. Add flour mixture; stir until just
moistened, do not over-mix. Fold in raisins and cranberries. Pour into
prepared pan.

Bake about 1 hour and 15 minutes or until a wooden pick inserted in center
comes out clean. Remove from oven; cool in pan 10 minutes. Remove from
pan; cool completely on a rack. Refrigerate leftovers.

Makes 1 loaf.

DROP CRANBERRY SCONES

Both fresh and dried cranberries are used these scones.

2 cups all-purpose flour
⅓ cup granulated sugar
2 teaspoons baking powder
¼ teaspoon salt
6 tablespoons cold butter, cut up (no substitution)

½ cup fresh or frozen cranberries, coarsely chopped
⅓ cup dried cranberries

½ cup whole milk
½ teaspoon pure vanilla extract
1 large egg
1 tablespoon sugar

Preheat oven to 425°.
Grease a baking sheet.

In a food processor, pulse first five ingredients until mixture resembles fine meal; transfer to a large bowl. Stir in all cranberries.

Beat milk, vanilla and egg in a bowl with a fork. Add to flour mixture; stir with a fork until moistened. Drop dough by heaping teaspoonfuls 2 inches apart onto prepared baking sheet. Sprinkle with 1 tablespoon granulated sugar.

Bake 12–14 minutes or until golden. Cool on a wire rack.

Makes 12 scones.

ORANGE-CRANBERRY SCONES

These are great for breakfast…serve warm.

2¼ cups all-purpose flour
3 tablespoons granulated sugar
1 tablespoon baking powder
2½ teaspoons freshly grated
   orange peel
⅛ cup cold butter
½ cup Mandarin orange
   segments, chopped

½ cup sweetened dried
   cranberries, chopped
1 cup dairy sour cream
1 egg
2 tablespoons orange juice
1 teaspoon pure vanilla extract
1 tablespoon granulated sugar

Preheat oven to 400°.
Grease a 9-inch round cake pan.

Mix flour, 3 tablespoons sugar, baking powder and orange peel. Cut in butter until mixture resembles coarse crumbs. Stir in Mandarin oranges and cranberries.

In another bowl, mix sour cream, egg, orange juice and vanilla; beat until smooth. Stir into flour mixture until well mixed.

Spread batter into prepared pan. Sprinkle top with 1 tablespoon sugar.

Bake 28–32 minutes or until a wooden pick inserted in center comes out clean and scone is lightly browned. Cool 5 minutes in pan; remove from pan and cut into wedges. Refrigerate leftovers.

Makes 8 scones.

DRIED CRANBERRY BISCUITS

Serve warm with favorite spread.

2 cups all-purpose flour
1 tablespoon baking powder
½ cup corn oil
¾ cup milk
¼ cup sweetened dried cranberries

2 tablespoons granulated sugar mixed
with ½ teaspoon ground cinnamon in a cup

Preheat oven to 400°.
Spray a baking sheet with cooking spray.

Mix flour and baking powder. Stir in corn oil; mix until coarse crumbs form.
Stir in milk to form a soft dough. Stir in cranberries.

With floured hands, form dough into a ball, then press dough onto prepared
baking sheet. Press evenly into a 6x6-inch square. Cut dough into 12 biscuits,
but do not separate them. Sprinkle with sugar-cinnamon mixture.

Bake 15–20 minutes or until lightly browned.

Makes 12 biscuits.

EASY CRANBERRY DROP BISCUITS

Serve warm with softened butter and honey.

2¼ cups prepared all-purpose baking mix
⅔ cup whole milk
½ cup chopped sweetened dried cranberries
½ cup chopped nuts
2 tablespoons granulated sugar

Preheat oven to 450°.
Stir all ingredients to form a soft dough. Drop dough by spoonfuls onto an ungreased baking sheet.

Bake 8–10 minutes or until golden brown. Remove from oven.

Makes 10 biscuits.

Appetizers

CHEESE WITH CRANBERRIES

A delicious appetizer. Serve with crackers.

1 8-ounce package cream cheese
¼ cup crumbled blue cheese
1 cup shredded white cheddar cheese
1 tablespoon chopped onion

1 cup cranberries, thawed if using frozen
¼ cup granulated sugar
3 tablespoons frozen apple juice concentrate, thawed
2 tablespoons red wine (optional)

Process cheeses and onion in a food processor until well blended. Spoon mixture into a 1½-cup flat shallow dish lined with plastic food wrap. Cover and refrigerate.

Cook cranberries, sugar and apple juice concentrate in a small saucepan over low heat, stirring often, until cranberries pop; continue cooking until mixture thickens slightly, about 3 minutes. Remove from heat. Stir in wine (if desired). Refrigerate until cooled.

Remove cheese mix from refrigerator 20 minutes before serving; invert on a serving plate; remove plastic. Top with cranberry mixture; serve. Refrigerate leftovers.

Makes 12 servings.

CRANBERRY BRIE APPETIZER

Warm cheese and chutney…a good starter. Serve with crackers.

1 16-ounce round Brie
⅔ cup cranberry chutney (see pg. 216)
4 bacon slices, cooked and crumbled
¼ cup sliced green onions

Remove rind from top of cheese, cutting to within 1-inch from outside edge. Place Brie on a microwave-safe plate. Top with chutney; microwave on high one minute or until cheese softens. Do not melt the cheese. Remove from oven; sprinkle with bacon and onions. Refrigerate leftovers.

Makes 14 servings.

CRANBERRY COCKTAIL MEATBALLS

Place in a chafing dish to keep warm.

1 16-ounce can jellied cranberry sauce
1 12-ounce bottle chili sauce
1 teaspoon ground cumin
¼ teaspoon cayenne pepper, or to taste

2 1-pound bags frozen cocktail meatballs

Stir all ingredients except meatballs in a large saucepan over medium heat until smooth.

Add meatballs. Cook over medium-low heat, stirring occasionally, until meatballs are thoroughly heated, about 12 minutes. Refrigerate leftovers.

Makes 30 servings.

CRANBERRY-GLAZED
HAM BALLS AND SMOKIES

Serve with toothpicks.

1 egg, beaten
½ cup finely crushed crackers
¼ cup minced onion
2 tablespoons snipped dried cranberries
  (snip into pieces with kitchen scissors)
2 tablespoons milk
pinch of ground cloves
½ pound ground pork
½ pound ground fully cooked ham

1 16-ounce package small fully cooked smoked sausage links

1 16-ounce can jellied cranberry sauce
1 12-ounce bottle chili sauce
1 tablespoon white vinegar
¼ teaspoon dry mustard

Preheat oven to 350°.
Combine the first eight ingredients, mix well. Form into 50 meatballs. Place meatballs on a lightly greased 15x10x1-inch baking pan. Bake until no longer pink, about 15 minutes; drain and place into a 3½–5-quart crock pot. Add the cooked sausage links.

Stir the remaining ingredients in a saucepan over medium heat until cranberry sauce is melted. Pour sauce over meatballs and sausage. Cover and cook on high-heat setting for 2–3 hours. Serve immediately.

Makes 25 appetizers.

CRANBERRY PIZZA APPETIZER

A nice party treat.

1 8-ounce can refrigerated crescent dinner rolls
1 8-ounce package Brie cheese, rind removed,
 cut into ½-inch cubes
¾ cup canned whole berry cranberry sauce
½ cup chopped pecans

Preheat oven to 425°.
Unroll dough and separate into triangles; place on a lightly greased
12-inch pizza pan with tips toward center. Press out dough with hands.
Bake about 6 minutes or until light golden brown.

Remove from oven. Sprinkle with cheese and spoon cranberry evenly over
cheese. Sprinkle with pecans. Return to oven; bake until cheese is melted
and crust is golden brown, about 8 minutes. Remove from oven; cool
slightly. Cut into wedges. Refrigerate leftovers.

Makes 8 servings.

CRANBERRY SWISS DIP

Serve with apple and pear wedges along with crackers.

1 8-ounce container soft cream cheese with pineapple
1½ cups shredded Swiss cheese (6 ounces)
½ cup sweetened dried cranberries
1 tablespoon grated orange peel
2 tablespoons apple juice

Preheat oven to 375°.
Mix all ingredients until well blended. Spread into an ungreased 9-inch pie plate. Bake until thoroughly heated, about 15 minutes.

Makes 8 servings.

GRILLED CRANBERRY SHRIMP

A tasty appetizer.

24 large shrimp, peeled and deveined
Italian dressing

2 cups cranberries, very finely chopped
¼ cup granulated sugar
⅓ cup prepared horseradish

Marinate shrimp in Italian dressing in a glass bowl in the refrigerator for one hour. Place shrimp on skewers.

Mix cranberries and sugar in a saucepan. Cook over medium heat, stirring constantly, until mixture is well blended, about 2 minutes. Remove from heat; stir in horseradish.

Baste shrimp with cranberry-horseradish sauce. Grill 3–4 minutes (depending on size). Turn shrimp over; baste with cranberry-horseradish sauce, and grill another 3–4 minutes.

Makes 12 appetizers.

Salads
Soups

BLACK CHERRY-CRANBERRY GELATIN SALAD

Serve in a lettuce cup.

1 6-ounce package black cherry flavor gelatin
2 cups boiling water
1 16-ounce can whole berry cranberry sauce
1 16-ounce container dairy sour cream
1 cup chopped walnuts

In a large glass bowl, stir gelatin and boiling water until dissolved. Stir in cranberry sauce; mix well. Stir in sour cream until blended. Chill mixture until slightly thickened but not set. Stir in walnuts. Refrigerate until set. Store in refrigerator.

Makes 10 servings.

CRANBERRY-RASPBERRY SHERBET SALAD

Garnish this salad with sugared cranberries when serving.

1 3-ounce package raspberry flavor gelatin
1 3-ounce package lemon flavor gelatin
1 cup boiling water
1 8-ounce carton dairy sour cream
2 cups raspberry sherbet
1 cup fresh cranberry relish (see pg. 222) or
   purchased cranberry-orange relish

Dissolve both gelatins in boiling water in a bowl. Beat in sour cream with a wire whisk until smooth. Stir in sherbet until blended. Chill until partially set. Stir in cranberry relish. Spoon mixture into a 5-cup mold. Cover and chill until firm, about 6 hours. Unmold on a lettuce-lined serving platter. Store in refrigerator.

Makes 8 servings.

HUE'S CRANBERRY ICE CREAM SALAD

A refreshing summer-time salad.

1 3-ounce package orange flavor gelatin
1 cup boiling water, mixed with 1 tablespoon fresh lemon juice
1 pint vanilla ice cream
2 large oranges, peeled and diced
2 teaspoons freshly grated orange peel
1 16-ounce can cranberry sauce

Dissolve gelatin in boiling water mixture in a bowl. Stir in ice cream until blended. Fold in orange, orange peel and cranberry sauce. Pour into a mold and refrigerate until firm. Store in refrigerator.

Makes 8 servings.

LAYERED PEAR-CRANBERRY CREAM CHEESE MOLD

Pears, cream cheese and tangy cranberries in this salad.

1 6-ounce package lime flavor gelatin
1½ cups boiling water
1½ cups cold ginger ale
2 tablespoons fresh lemon juice
1 16-ounce can pear halves, drained and chopped

1 8-ounce package cream cheese, softened
¼ cup dried cranberries
¼ cup chopped pecans

Dissolve gelatin in boiling water in a bowl. Stir in cold ginger ale and lemon juice. Pour 1 cup gelatin mixture into a 5-cup mold. Refrigerate until slightly thickened but not set. Place half the pears in mold, pushing into gelatin.

In a bowl, add remaining gelatin to cream cheese; whisk with wire whisk until blended. Refrigerate until slightly thickened; stir in remaining pears, cranberries and pecans; spoon over gelatin layer in mold. Refrigerate until firm. Unmold on serving plate. Store in refrigerator.

Makes 10 servings.

MANDARIN-CRANBERRY SALAD

Top with a little sour cream when serving, if desired.

3½ cups cranberry juice cocktail, divided
1 6-ounce package orange flavor gelatin
1½ cups chopped fresh or frozen cranberries
½ cup chopped walnuts
1 11-ounce can Mandarin orange segments, drained

Bring1½ cups cranberry juice cocktail to a boil in a small saucepan; pour into a large bowl. Add gelatin; stir until dissolved. Stir in remaining 2 cups cold cranberry juice cocktail. Refrigerate until partially thickened but not set, about 1 hour. Stir cranberries, walnuts and orange segments into thickened gelatin.

Pour mixture into a lightly oiled 6-cup ring or mold. Refrigerate until firm, about 4 hours. Unmold unto lettuce-lined serving plate. Store in refrigerator.

Makes 8 servings.

MOOSE'S CRANBERRY SALAD

A good side to serve with ham or turkey.

2 3-ounce packages cranberry flavor gelatin
2 cups boiling water
1 16-ounce can whole berry cranberry sauce
1 20-ounce can crushed pineapple in juice
1 6-ounce frozen orange juice concentrate, undiluted, thawed
½ cup chopped pecans

Dissolve gelatin in boiling water in a bowl. Stir in remaining ingredients until well mixed. Refrigerate until set. Store in refrigerator.

Makes 6 servings.

RASPBERRY-CRANBERRY SALAD

Salad and relish in one!

1 6-ounce package raspberry flavor gelatin
1½ cups boiling water
½ cup ginger ale
juice of 1 fresh lemon
grated rind of half a fresh lemon
1 10-ounce package frozen raspberries
1 10-ounce package frozen cranberry-orange relish
1 8-ounce carton dairy sour cream

Dissolve gelatin in boiling water in a bowl. Add remaining ingredients except sour cream. Pour half the mixture into a large ring mold. Refrigerate until set. Spread sour cream over chilled mixture; chill about one hour. Add remaining mixture; refrigerate overnight. Unmold onto a lettuce-lined serving platter. Store in refrigerator.

Makes 12 servings.

RAW CRANBERRY-ORANGE MOLD

A creamy orange dressing tops this cranberry salad.

Salad
1 6-ounce package strawberry flavor gelatin
1 cup granulated sugar
1½ cups boiling water
1½ cups cold water
2 cups fresh cranberries, coarsely chopped
1 large orange, coarsely chopped

Dressing
1 8-ounce package cream cheese, softened
1 tablespoon granulated sugar
⅓ cup fresh orange juice
1 teaspoons freshly grated orange rind
½ teaspoon pure vanilla extract

Salad: Dissolve gelatin and sugar in boiling water in a bowl. Stir in cold water; chill until partially set. Fold in cranberries and chopped orange. Pour mixture into a 1½-quart mold or glass baking dish. Refrigerate until set, about 8 hours. Top each serving with a spoonful of dressing. Store in refrigerator.

Dressing: Beat cream cheese and sugar in a glass bowl. Stir in remaining ingredients until well-blended. Refrigerate.

Makes 12 servings.

RUTH'S CRANBERRY SALAD

A good salad to offer with cold turkey sandwiches.

1 6-ounce package cherry flavor gelatin
2 cups boiling water
1 16-ounce can whole berry cranberry sauce
1 20-ounce can crushed pineapple with juice,
  drained, reserving ¼ cup juice
1 8-ounce package cream cheese, softened
1 tablespoon mayonnaise
1 cup chopped pecans

Dissolve gelatin in boiling water in a bowl. Stir in cranberries and pineapple. Pour half of the mixture in a bowl and let stand at room temperature. Refrigerate the other half until firm.

In another bowl, mix cream cheese, mayonnaise, reserved pineapple juice and pecans until well blended. Spread mixture over chilled gelatin. Refrigerate 10 minutes. Pour the room temperature gelatin over top of cream cheese layer. Refrigerate until set. Store in refrigerator.

Makes 8 servings.

STRAWBERRY-CRANBERRY GELATIN SALAD

Garnish with whipped cream when serving, if desired.

1 6-ounce package strawberry flavor gelatin
1 cup boiling water
1 16-ounce can whole berry cranberry sauce
1 16-ounce package frozen strawberries
½ cup finely diced celery
¼ cup finely chopped nuts
1 8-ounce package cream cheese, softened, cut into small pieces

Mix gelatin with boiling water until dissolved in a bowl. Refrigerate to chill slightly. Stir in cranberry sauce, strawberries, celery and nuts. Fold in cream cheese. Pour mixture into an 8-inch square baking dish. Store in refrigerator.

Makes 8 servings.

BROCCOLI WITH CRANBERRIES SALAD

Serve with crisp bread sticks.

Salad
5 cups broccoli florets, cut into ½-inch pieces
½ red onion, thinly sliced
1 cup shredded sharp cheddar cheese
1 cup crumbled cooked bacon
1 cup sweetened dried cranberries
1 cup shelled sunflower seeds

Dressing
1 cup mayonnaise
3 tablespoons granulated sugar
2 tablespoons red wine vinegar
½ teaspoon salt
¼ teaspoon freshly ground black pepper

Mix all salad ingredients in a large salad bowl.

In a small bowl, beat all dressing ingredients with a wire whisk until blended; spoon over salad, and toss to mix well. Refrigerate 1 hour before serving. Refrigerate leftovers.

Makes 6 servings.

CARROT-CRANBERRY-RAISIN SALAD

Serve this salad on lettuce leaves.

4 cups peeled shredded fresh carrots
½ cup sweetened dried cranberries
½ cup dark raisins
½ cup crushed pineapple
¾ cup mayonnaise

Mix all ingredients in a bowl. Chill. Refrigerate leftovers.

Makes 8 servings.

CRANBERRY CHICKEN SALAD

Serve with warm hard rolls and softened butter.

1 cup dairy sour cream
½ cup mayonnaise
1 tablespoon cider vinegar
1 teaspoon salt
1 teaspoon granulated sugar
ground white pepper to taste

4 cups cooked diced chicken breast
2 cups seedless green grapes
1 cup cashews
½ cup fresh cranberries, halved

Mix first six ingredients in a large glass bowl until well blended.

Add remaining ingredients; mix well. Refrigerate and chill before serving. Refrigerate leftovers.

Makes 4 servings.

CRANBERRY WALDORF SALAD

Waldorf salad, an all-time favorite.

Dressing
⅔ cup whole cranberry sauce
¼ cup mayonnaise
¼ cup dairy sour cream
¼ cup whole milk
2 teaspoons fresh lemon juice
¼ teaspoon celery seed

Salad
4 cups chopped apples
1 cup seedless grapes, halved
1 cup sliced celery
⅔ cup broken pecans, toasted
½ cup raisins

Dressing: combine all ingredients, set aside.

Combine all salad ingredients in a bowl. Spoon mixture on lettuce-lined salad plates. Drizzle with salad dressing. Refrigerate leftovers.

Makes 10 servings.

CURRIED CHICKEN CRANBERRY SALAD

Good for sandwiches too…diced apple and celery.

¾ cup mayonnaise
2 teaspoons lime juice
¾ teaspoon curry powder
2 cups cubed cooked chicken breast
1 medium apple, cored, cut into bite-size pieces
¾ cup sweetened dried cranberries
½ cup thinly sliced celery
¼ cup chopped pecans
3 green onions, thinly sliced
lettuce

In a large glass serving bowl, mix mayonnaise, lime juice and curry powder until well blended. Stir in remaining ingredients until coated. Cover and chill well before serving. Serve on a bed of shredded leaf lettuce. Refrigerate leftovers.

Makes 4 servings.

DORIE'S CRANBERRY FLUFF

Thanks, cousin Dorie.

2 cups fresh cranberries, ground
3 cups miniature marshmallows
¾ cup granulated sugar
2 cups diced, unpeeled apples
1 cup seedless green grapes
⅓ cup chopped nuts
1 cup pineapple chunks, halved
1 cup heavy cream, whipped

Combine cranberries, marshmallows and sugar in a glass bowl. Cover and refrigerate overnight. Stir in apples, grapes, nuts and pineapple. Fold in whipped cream. Chill. Refrigerate leftovers.

Makes 8 servings.

DRIED CRANBERRY FETA CHEESE SALAD

The dried cranberries add a little tang to this salad!

1 10-ounce package mixed salad greens
1 cup sweetened dried cranberries
1 4-ounce package crumbled feta cheese
½ cup broken walnuts, toasted

2 tablespoons balsamic vinegar
1 tablespoon honey
1 teaspoon Dijon style mustard
¼ teaspoon freshly ground black pepper
¼ cup extra virgin olive oil

In a large serving bowl, toss salad greens, cranberries, cheese and walnuts.

In another bowl, whisk vinegar, honey, mustard and pepper with a wire whisk until well blended. Gradually whisk in olive oil until blended. Pour dressing over salad; toss until coated. Serve immediately or refrigerate.

Makes 6 servings.

FROZEN PINEAPPLE-CRANBERRY SALAD

Bev sends this recipe from Perley, Minnesota.

3 cups fresh cranberries, ground
1 8-ounce can crushed pineapple in juice, undrained
1½ cups granulated sugar
½ cup chopped pecans
1 8-ounce package cream cheese, softened
1 8-ounce container frozen non-dairy whipped topping, thawed

Combine cranberries, pineapple, sugar and pecans; let stand 10 minutes. Gradually stir in cream cheese. Fold in thawed whipped topping. Pour mixture into a lightly buttered 13x9x2-inch glass baking dish. Cover and freeze. Cut into squares. Freeze leftovers.

For Variation: Replace the 8-ounce can crushed pineapple with one 20-ounce can crushed pineapple. Use 1 cup sugar only. Replace cream cheese with 1 package small marshmallows. Let stand overnight; add the thawed whipped topping, and then freeze. Cut into squares, freeze leftovers.

Makes 12 servings.

POMEGRANATE-CRANBERRY SALAD

A colorful salad for the holidays.

Salad
1 bunch romaine, torn into bite-size pieces
1 cup fresh pomegranate seeds
½ cup dried cranberries
½ medium red onion, sliced

Dressing
½ cup mayonnaise
⅓ cup granulated sugar
¼ cup milk
2 tablespoons white vinegar
1 tablespoon poppy seeds

Place salad ingredients in a large glass salad bowl.

Place all dressing ingredients in a small bowl; beat with a wire whisk until well blended; pour over salad; toss. Serve immediately or refrigerate.

Makes 6 servings.

ROASTED TURKEY CRANBERRY SALAD

A good luncheon salad…serve with warm rolls.

1 cup whole berry cranberry sauce
2 tablespoons white vinegar
1 tablespoon granulated sugar
1 cup crumbled feta cheese, divided
½ cup salad oil

red lettuce
16 slices cold roasted turkey breast
½ cup coarsely chopped pecans

In a blender, blend cranberry sauce, vinegar, sugar and ½ cup feta cheese on high speed a few seconds. With blender running, slowly add oil through hole in lid of blender cap. Spoon dressing into a glass container. Stir in remaining feta cheese. Refrigerate leftovers.

Line individual salad plates with lettuce leaves. Place 4 slices turkey on each. Sprinkle with pecans. Drizzle with salad dressing. Serve immediately. Refrigerate leftovers.

Makes 4 servings.

SANDRA'S CRANBERRY SALAD

Simple to prepare…delicious with turkey or chicken.

1 16-ounce can whole berry cranberry sauce
1 8-ounce can crushed pineapple, drained
½ cup chopped pecans

Mix all ingredients in a serving bowl.

Makes 4 servings.

SMOKED TURKEY STRAWBERRY-CRANBERRY SALAD

Serve with bread sticks or hard rolls.

Dressing
1 cup dairy sour cream
¼ cup honey
2 tablespoons chopped fresh flat parsley
½ teaspoon ground mustard
⅛ teaspoon ground black pepper
3 tablespoons fresh lemon juice

Salad
4 cups smoked turkey, cut into thin strips
8 ounces provolone cheese, cubed
2 cups thinly sliced celery
1 cup honey-roasted cashews
½ cup sweetened dried cranberries

3 cups fresh strawberries
fresh mixed salad greens

In a large salad bowl, mix all dressing ingredients until blended.

Add all salad ingredients except strawberries and salad greens; toss. Add strawberries; toss gently to coat. Line individual salad plates with mixed salad greens; top with salad. Refrigerate leftovers.

Makes 8 servings.

STRAWBERRY-CRANBERRY SLAW

If the slaw is served immediately without chilling 8 hours, you will have 8 servings. The slaw will condense when chilled 8 hours.

6 cups thinly sliced green cabbage
1½ cups sliced fresh strawberries
½ cup dried cranberries
¼ cup raspberry-flavor vinegar
¼ cup cranberry juice cocktail
½ teaspoon salt
½ teaspoon white pepper

Mix all ingredients in a glass bowl; stir well. Serve immediately or cover and chill 8 hours, stirring occasionally. Store in refrigerator.

Makes 4–8 servings.

TURKEY WITH CRANBERRIES SALAD

Top this good salad with toasted sliced almonds when serving.

Salad
3 cups shredded cooked turkey
1 cup green seedless grapes, halved
1 cup thinly sliced celery
4 green onions, sliced
6 slices bacon, diced, cooked and drained
½ cup dried cranberries

Dressing
¾ cup mayonnaise
½ cup mango chutney
1 tablespoon fresh lemon juice
1 teaspoon curry powder
2 tablespoons minced chives
freshly ground black pepper to taste

lettuce, shredded

In a large bowl, combine all salad ingredients.

In a small bowl, whisk all dressing ingredients until blended. Pour dressing over turkey salad; toss to coat. Serve on a bed of shredded lettuce. Refrigerate leftovers.

Makes 6 servings.

WILD RICE CRANBERRY SALAD

The cherry tomato and sprout garnish adds color and texture.

1 cup wild rice
4 cups water

¼ cup chopped flat parsley
½ cup chopped celery
½ cup chopped green onions
½ cup sweetened dried cranberries
⅛ teaspoon ground black pepper

Dressing
½ cup cranberry juice
1 teaspoon dried basil
½ cup white vinegar
⅓ cup olive oil
½ teaspoon granulated sugar, or to taste
salt to taste

romaine lettuce, shredded
cherry tomatoes
alfalfa sprouts

In a saucepan, cook rice in water until tender but not mushy, about 45 minutes.
Drain well; cool. Place in a serving bowl. Add remaining salad ingredients.

In a small bowl, mix dressing ingredients. Add to salad mixture; mix well.
Serve on a bed of shredded romaine lettuce. Garnish with cherry tomatoes
and alfalfa sprouts. Refrigerate leftovers.

Makes 6 servings.

CHILLED CRANBERRY SOUP

For extra flavor, sprinkle sour cream with a pinch of nutmeg.

3 cups water
1½ cups granulated sugar
2 cinnamon sticks
¼ teaspoon ground cloves
4 cups fresh cranberries

2 tablespoon fresh lemon juice
1 tablespoon freshly grated orange rind
sour cream

Mix water, sugar, cinnamon sticks and cloves in a 4-quart saucepan. Bring to a boil over high heat. Add cranberries and return to a boil. Reduce heat; cook until cranberries pop, about 5 minutes.

Remove from heat. Stir in lemon juice and orange rind. Cool to room temperature. Chill in refrigerator 4 hours. Serve with a dollop of sour cream. Refrigerate leftovers.

Makes 4 servings.

CRANBERRY-TOPPED BUTTERNUT SQUASH-SWEET POTATO SOUP

A tasty soup.

Cranberry purée
⅓ cup water
¼ cup granulated sugar
1 cup fresh cranberries
2 tablespoons orange juice

Soup
1 tablespoon butter
1 large onion, sliced
4 cups low-sodium
   chicken broth, divided
1½ pounds peeled and
      cubed butternut squash

½ pound peeled and
   cubed sweet potato
2 large carrots, peeled and sliced
1½ teaspoons dried sage,
   crumbled
½ teaspoon ground mace
½ teaspoon ground ginger

½ teaspoon hot pepper sauce
salt to taste

Stir water and sugar in a saucepan until dissolved. Add cranberries; cook over medium heat, stirring occasionally, until cranberries pop, about 10 minutes. Cool slightly, then purée with orange juice in blender; set aside.

Heat butter in a large saucepan. Add onion; stir and cook over medium heat until golden brown. Add 2 cups broth and rest of soup ingredients. Bring to a boil; cover and cook on low heat until vegetables are tender, about 25 minutes.

Purée mixture in food processor in batches, pulsing until smooth. Return purée to saucepan. Whisk in remaining broth. Season with hot pepper sauce and salt; simmer gently.

Ladle hot soup into bowls, drop cranberry purée by spoonful on top, and swirl with a knife. Refrigerate leftover soup and cranberry purée.

Makes 8 servings.

CRANBERRY VEGETABLE SOUP

A hearty soup.

1 cup fresh cranberries
2 cups chopped onion
6 cups boiling water
6 beef bouillon cubes
1 cup sliced carrots
1 cup diced celery
2 cups diced peeled potatoes
1 cup frozen peas
1 cup cut green beans
1 16-ounce can whole tomatoes, chopped
2 teaspoons granulated sugar

Mix all ingredients in a 5-quart pot. Cover and simmer, stirring occasionally, 50 minutes. Add more water if needed.

Makes 6 servings.

Meals Paired with Cranberries

APPLE-CRANBERRY FRENCH TOAST

Assemble this breakfast treat the night before…bake in the morning.

1 cup brown sugar
½ cup butter, melted
2 teaspoons ground cinnamon, divided

3 tart apples, such as Granny Smith, peeled, cored and thinly sliced
½ cup sweetened dried cranberries
¼ cup raisins
1 loaf Italian or French bread, cut into 1-inch slices

6 large eggs
1½ cups whole milk
1 tablespoon pure vanilla extract

Mix brown sugar, butter and 1 teaspoon cinnamon in a 13x9-inch baking dish. Add apples, cranberries and raisins; toss until coated, then spread evenly over bottom of baking dish. Arrange slices of bread on top.

Mix eggs, milk, vanilla and 1 teaspoon cinnamon until well blended. Pour mixture over bread, soaking bread completely. Cover and refrigerate 4–12 hours. Cover with aluminum baking foil, and bake in a preheated 375° oven 40 minutes. Uncover and bake 5 minutes. Remove from oven; let stand 5 minutes before serving. Refrigerate leftovers.

Makes 12 servings.

CRANBERRY AND CHEESE GRILL

Serve with chips and favorite drink.

1 cup whole berry cranberry sauce
1 teaspoon prepared horseradish

8 slices sourdough bread
8 1-ounce slices deli turkey breast
8 slices deli American cheese
⅓ cup butter, melted

In a small bowl, mix cranberry sauce and horseradish. Divide the cranberry sauce mixture equally among 4 slices of the bread.

Place two slices turkey and two slices cheese on top of cranberry mixture; top each with another slice of bread. Brush top and bottom of each sandwich with melted butter.

Heat skillet or griddle on medium high heat. Place 2 sandwiches in skillet. Cook, turning once, until golden brown, about 6 minutes. Repeat with remaining sandwiches.

Makes 4 servings.

CRANBERRY CHICKEN BAKE

Serve with hot cooked regular long grain white rice along with a crisp green salad.

1 16-ounce can whole berry cranberry sauce
1 cup Russian salad dressing with honey, or French dressing
1 envelope onion soup mix (such as Lipton)
1 2½-pound chicken, cut into serving pieces
salt and ground black pepper

Mix cranberry sauce, salad dressing and soup mix in a bowl. Place chicken in a single layer into a 13x9x2-inch baking dish. Pour cranberry mixture over chicken. Cover and marinate in refrigerator several hours.

Preheat oven to 350°.
Remove cover from baking dish. Bake chicken uncovered about 1½ hours or until chicken tests done, stirring the glaze and basting chicken occasionally during cooking period. Serve chicken and glaze immediately. Refrigerate leftovers.

Makes 4 servings.

CRANBERRY-GLAZED HAM

Serve with scalloped potatoes, buttered peas and a green salad.

1 16-ounce can cranberry sauce, whole berry or jellied
½ cup apricot preserves
2 tablespoons sweet honey mustard

1 8-pound fully cooked whole boneless ham

Preheat oven to 325°.
In a saucepan, over medium heat, cook and stir cranberry sauce, preserves and mustard until preserves are melted and sauce is smooth. Remove from heat and set aside.

Place ham on a rack in a shallow roasting pan. Insert meat thermometer in thickest part of ham. Bake uncovered for about 2 hours or until thermometer registers 140°. Baste generously with cranberry glaze during the last 45 minutes of baking.

Makes 12 servings.

CRANBERRY HONEY-GLAZED PORK LOIN ROAST

Serve with garlic mashed potatoes and steamed broccoli.

1 16-ounce can whole berry or jellied cranberry sauce
¼ cup honey
2 tablespoons soy sauce
1 tablespoon sesame seeds
pinch ground ginger (optional)

¼ teaspoon salt
¼ teaspoon ground black pepper
¼ teaspoon garlic powder

1 3-pound boneless pork loin roast

Preheat oven to 325°.

In a small saucepan, over medium heat, stir first five ingredients until sauce is smooth. Remove from heat; set aside.

Season roast with salt, black pepper and garlic powder. Place roast into a 13x9-inch roasting pan. Bake uncovered until a meat thermometer registers 170°, about 1½–2 hours. Baste roast with glaze during the last 30 minutes of baking. Refrigerate leftovers.

Makes 8 servings

CRANBERRY MUSTARD-SAUCED CHICKEN TENDERLOINS

Serve over hot cooked regular long grain white rice. A green salad will complete this tasty meal.

1 pound chicken tenderloins, lightly seasoned
   with salt and ground black pepper
all-purpose flour
2 tablespoons butter, divided
2 tablespoons corn oil, divided

1 cup chicken broth
⅓ cup dry white wine
3 tablespoons Dijon mustard
1½ teaspoons cornstarch, mixed with 1½ tablespoons cold water
½ cup sweetened dried cranberries
¼ cup sliced green onion tops

Lightly coat chicken with flour. Heat half the butter and half the corn oil in a large skillet over medium heat. Add half the chicken; cook, turning once, until golden brown on each side and chicken is no longer pink. Remove to a deep serving platter; keep warm. Add and heat remaining butter and corn oil in skillet. Add remaining chicken; cook as before and remove to serving platter; keep warm.

Stir broth, wine and mustard in skillet. Add cornstarch mixture, stirring constantly. Stir in cranberries. Cook and stir until thickened. Stir in green onion tops. Pour warm sauce over warm chicken. Refrigerate leftovers.

Makes 4 servings.

CRANBERRY PANCAKES

Serve with soft butter and cranberry syrup.

1½ cups fresh cranberries, coarsely chopped
¼ cup granulated sugar
2 teaspoons finely shredded orange peel

1½ cups all-purpose flour
2 teaspoons baking powder
½ teaspoon baking soda
½ teaspoon salt

1 egg, slightly beaten
1 cup buttermilk
½ cup orange juice
3 tablespoons butter or margarine, melted

Mix cranberries, sugar and orange peel; set aside. In another bowl, mix flour, baking powder, baking soda and salt. In a third bowl, mix egg, buttermilk, orange juice and butter; add to flour mixture. Stir until just combined, batter should be lumpy. Fold in cranberry mixture.

Heat a lightly greased griddle or heavy skillet over medium heat. Pour about ¼ cup batter onto hot griddle for each pancake. Cook pancakes until golden brown; turn to cook other side. Serve hot.

Makes 16 pancakes.

CRANBERRY RIBS

Serve with crusty rolls, a creamy coleslaw and corn on the cob.

4 pounds pork spareribs or country-style ribs

2½ cups fresh cranberries
½ cup water
½ cup granulated sugar

1 cup brown sugar
½ cup chili sauce
6 tablespoons apple cider vinegar
¼ cup chopped onion
¼ cup Worcestershire sauce

Place ribs in a large saucepan with enough water to cover. Bring to a boil, then reduce heat; cover and simmer 30 minutes.

In a heavy saucepan, stir and cook cranberries, water and granulated sugar over medium high heat until cranberries pop, about 5 minutes. Place a sieve over a bowl. Pour cranberry mixture through sieve, pressing with back of spoon until no pulp is left; pour back into saucepan.

Add remaining ingredients except ribs to saucepan. Bring to a boil; reduce heat, and simmer, stirring often, until thickened, about 20 minutes.

Preheat oven to 350°.
Drain ribs; cut into individual portions. Place in a shallow baking dish. Pour sauce over ribs. Bake until tender, about 35–40 minutes.

Makes 4 servings.

CRANBERRY-SPICED COUSCOUS

A quick and delicious vegetarian main dish…serve with a green salad.

1 tablespoon margarine or butter
½ medium-size red onion, chopped
1 8-ounce package mushrooms, sliced

1 14-ounce can low-sodium vegetable broth
¼ cup water

1 15-ounce can low-sodium garbanzo beans
½ cup dried cranberries
½ cup golden raisins
¼ cup dry sherry
1 teaspoon salt
½ teaspoon ground cinnamon
¼ teaspoon ground black pepper
1 10-ounce package plain couscous

Melt margarine in a deep 12-inch saucepan over medium high heat. Add onion and mushrooms; cook and stir 3 minutes.

Bring broth and water to a boil in a 1-quart saucepan over high heat.

Stir beans, cranberries, raisins, sherry, salt, cinnamon and pepper into mushroom mixture. Remove from heat. Add couscous. Stir in hot broth. Cover and let stand until liquid is absorbed. Fluff with fork and serve.

Makes 4 servings.

CRANBERRY-STUFFED CABBAGE

Serve with warm rolls and butter.

1 head cabbage
1½ pounds ground beef
¼ cup long grain regular
  rice (not instant)
1 carrot, shredded
2 eggs, slightly beaten
1 cup chopped onion
1 rib celery, finely chopped
1 teaspoon salt
⅛ teaspoon garlic powder
⅛ teaspoon ground black pepper

1 tablespoon corn oil
1 medium onion, diced
1 16-ounce can whole tomatoes,
  chopped
1 cup fresh cranberries
1 16-ounce can whole
  berry cranberry sauce
1 teaspoon chicken
  bouillon granules

Core cabbage, remove leaves; cover leaves with boiling water until limp; drain.

In a bowl, mix beef, rice, carrot, eggs, 1 cup chopped onion, celery, salt, garlic powder and black pepper.

Heat corn oil in a large saucepan; stir and cook diced onion until golden. Add tomatoes, cranberries, cranberry sauce and bouillon. Bring to a boil, then reduce heat and simmer 5 minutes.

Place a portion of meat mixture on each large cabbage leaf. Roll and fold cabbage to enclose filling; carefully place rolls in sauce in saucepan. Cover and simmer 1½ hours.

Makes 6 servings.

CRANBERRY-STUFFED CHICKEN

To bake stuffing separately, place in a greased 1½-quart baking dish; cover and bake at 350° for 40 minutes. Refrigerate leftovers.

1 cup chopped celery
1 cup chopped onion
⅔ cup dried cranberries
½ cup butter
1 garlic clove, minced
3 cups herb-seasoned
    stuffing croutons
1 cup corn bread stuffing
    or crumbled corn bread
2 cups chicken broth,
    approximately

Salt mixture
½ teaspoon salt
½ teaspoon ground black pepper
¼ teaspoon poultry seasoning
¼ teaspoon rubbed sage

1 6–7-pound roasting chicken

2 tablespoons butter, melted

Preheat oven to 350°.
In a large saucepan, stir and cook celery, onion and cranberries in ½ cup butter until tender. Stir in garlic, croutons, stuffing and enough broth to moisten.

Combine all salt mixture ingredients. Place chicken breast side up on a rack in a roasting pan. Sprinkle chicken inside and outside with salt mixture. Loosely stuff with cranberry mixture. Brush chicken with melted butter.

Bake uncovered 2½–3 hours, or until juices run clear and a meat thermometer reads 180° for the chicken and 165° for the stuffing. Baste chicken occasionally while cooking. Refrigerate leftovers.

Makes 8 servings.

CRANBERRY-STUFFED PORK CHOPS

Serve with baked or mashed potatoes, buttered corn and a crisp green salad.

1 cup fresh cranberries
¼ cup orange marmalade
⅛ teaspoon ground cloves

4 pork loin chops, lightly seasoned with salt and pepper

4 tablespoons honey

Preheat oven to 325°.
Mix cranberries, marmalade and cloves.

Cut a pocket in each pork chop. Fill pockets with cranberry mixture. Place in a greased baking pan. Spoon 1 tablespoon honey over each pork chop. Bake uncovered until meat is no longer pink in center, about 45 minutes. Refrigerate leftovers.

Makes 4 servings.

FRESH CRANBERRY-STUFFED TURKEY

Serve with your traditional side dishes.

1 22-pound turkey

Stuffing
3 cups fresh cranberries
¾ cup granulated sugar
1½ cups fresh orange juice
9 cups dried bread cubes
1 cup butter, melted
3 cups sliced celery
1 cup chopped onion
2 teaspoons salt
½ teaspoon ground black pepper
¼ teaspoon allspice

Sauce
½ cup fresh orange juice
2 10-ounce packages frozen
  cranberry-orange sauce

Stuffing: Cook cranberries, sugar and 1½ cups orange juice over medium heat, stirring occasionally, until cranberries pop and sugar is dissolved, about 10 minutes. Cool 15 minutes. Mix all remaining stuffing ingredients; stir in cooled cranberry mixture.

Preheat oven to 325°.
Stuff turkey. Place turkey on a rack in a roasting pan. Bake as directed on turkey package or about 5–6 hours. Meat thermometer placed in thigh without touching the bone should read 180°, and stuffing should read 170°.

Sauce: Stir sauce ingredients over medium high heat until melted. Baste turkey with sauce during last 30 minutes of cooking. Bring remaining sauce to a boil in another saucepan; serve over turkey. Refrigerate leftovers.

Makes 8 servings.

LEFTOVER TURKEY
CRANBERRY SANDWICH

Serve with potato chips, pickles and leftover olives.

sliced leftover turkey breast
leftover bread dressing
mayonnaise
cranberry sauce
salt and black pepper
2 slices white bread, buttered

Put it together and go for it.

Makes 1 sandwich.

ROASTED QUAIL WITH
CRANBERRY PECAN STUFFING

If desired, substitute Cornish hens and prepare the same as quails.

**8 quails, dressed, seasoned
with ½ teaspoon salt and
½ teaspoon pepper**
**⅓ cup fresh orange juice, mixed
with ¼ cup melted butter**

Glaze
1½ cups cranberry juice
1¼ cups granulated sugar
**1½ cups fresh or frozen
cranberries**
**1½ teaspoons grated fresh
orange rind**

Stuffing
2 tablespoon butter
½ cup diced onion
2 ribs celery, diced
¾ cup chopped pecans, toasted
⅓ cup orange sections, chopped
⅓ cup chopped cranberries
1 tablespoon granulated sugar
**2 slices white bread, toasted
and cubed**
**⅓ teaspoon each: salt, dried
thyme, rubbed sage**
1 large egg, slightly beaten
2 tablespoons fresh orange juice

Glaze: Stir and cook cranberry juice and sugar over medium heat until mixture thickens, about 25 minutes. Add cranberries and orange rind; cook and stir 2 minutes or until cranberries pop. Remove from heat; let cool; set aside.

Stuffing: Melt butter over medium heat; add onion and celery; cook and stir until tender. Stir in pecans, orange sections, cranberries and sugar; remove from heat. Mix bread and spices; add to cranberry mixture. Stir in egg and orange juice.

Preheat oven to 325°.
Spoon about ¼ cup stuffing into each quail; tie legs together with string; place in shallow roasting pan. Brush with orange juice mixture. Bake for 1 hour, basting quail with orange juice mixture every 15 minutes. If necessary to brown, broil 5½ inches from heat 3–4 minutes. Serve immediately with cranberry glaze. Refrigerate leftovers.

Makes 4 servings.

TURKEY CRANBERRY BAGEL

A little extra tang in this bagel.

½ cup chopped celery
½ cup chopped dried cranberries
⅓ cup mayonnaise
1 tablespoon Dijon-style mustard

4 bagels, split
½ pound thinly sliced deli turkey breast
4 slices deli American cheese
4 lettuce leaves

Stir together first four ingredients; refrigerate at least 1 hour.

Spoon cranberry mixture equally on bagel halves. Layer each bottom bagel half with equal amount of turkey, cheese and lettuce; add bagel top.

Makes 4 sandwiches.

TURKEY CRANBERRY WRAPS

Serve with assorted pickles and favorite beverage.

4 10-inch flour tortillas
¾ cup whole berry cranberry sauce
2 tablespoons spicy brown mustard

2 cups chopped cooked turkey
¼ cup chopped pecans, toasted
2 green onions, diced
2 tablespoons minced crystallized ginger
2 cups shredded lettuce

Heat tortillas using package directions. Mix cranberry sauce and mustard; spoon mixture evenly down center of each tortilla.

Mix turkey, pecans, onions and ginger; spoon evenly over cranberry mixture. Top each evenly with lettuce and roll up. Serve.

Makes 4 servings.

VENISON WITH CRANBERRIES

Serve with wild rice pilaf along with a wilted lettuce salad.

3 pounds venison leg roast

Seasoning
¼ cup olive oil
2 teaspoons coarsely
   ground black pepper
2 teaspoons dried thyme
   leaves, crushed
1 teaspoon ground
   juniper berries
½ teaspoon salt

¼ cup corn oil

Spice bag
cheesecloth
1 3-inch cinnamon stick
4 teaspoons whole cloves
4 teaspoons fennel seeds
4 teaspoons black peppercorns

Sauce
5 cups fresh cranberries
1½ cups red wine
¾ cup balsamic vinegar
½ cup granulated sugar
¾ cup frozen orange
   juice concentrate, undiluted

Seasoning: Mix all ingredients and rub on venison roast.
Cover roast and refrigerate overnight. Bring to room temperature. In a large skillet, heat corn oil. Brown venison on all sides. Place on a rack in a roasting pan. Bake about 50–60 minutes, to desired doneness. Remove from oven. Let stand at room temperature a few minutes before slicing. Serve with cranberry sauce. Refrigerate leftovers.

Spice bag: Combine all ingredients; tie in cheesecloth.

Sauce: Bring all ingredients to a boil in a heavy saucepan. Add spice bag. Reduce heat and simmer about 30 minutes or until cranberries are very soft. Discard spice bag.

Makes 8 servings.

Stuffing
Sides

CORNBREAD CRANBERRY
SAUSAGE DRESSING

Dressing can be made a day ahead of time...cover and refrigerate.

1 pound bulk pork sausage

2 cups chopped onion
2 cups chopped celery
8 cups crumbled baked cornbread
1 cup dried cranberries
½ cup chopped dried apricots

2 eggs, slightly beaten
½ teaspoon dried rubbed sage
½ cup butter or margarine, melted
salt and ground black pepper

¾ cup chicken broth,
   approximately

Preheat oven to 325°.
Crumble sausage into a 12-inch skillet. Cook and stir over medium-high heat until lightly browned. Place sausage in a large bowl.

Discard all but 2 tablespoons fat in skillet. Add onions to skillet; cook and stir until softened; add to bowl. Add remaining ingredients except broth to bowl; mix well. Add just enough chicken broth to lightly moisten dressing. Spoon dressing into a shallow 3-quart baking casserole.

Cover and bake until hot, about 25 minutes. Uncover; bake until top is lightly browned, about 20 minutes.

Makes 12 servings.

PECAN CRANBERRY STUFFING

This is enough stuffing for a 16-pound turkey.

⅓ cup butter or margarine
1½ cups thinly sliced celery
¾ cup chopped onion
1½ teaspoons dried sage, crushed
¾ teaspoon dried thyme, crushed
½ teaspoon ground black pepper

9 cups dry bread cubes
¾ cup chopped pecans
¾ cup dried cranberries
¾–1 cup chicken broth, approximately

Preheat oven to 325°.
Melt butter in a small saucepan. Add celery and onion; stir and cook until tender, about 5 minutes. Remove from heat. Stir in sage, thyme and pepper. Place bread cubes in a large bowl. Stir in celery mixture, pecans and cranberries. Drizzle with just enough chicken broth, tossing gently, to moisten, about ¾ cup. Spoon into a greased 3-quart baking dish.

Cover and bake about 45 minutes. Add a little more broth for a moist stuffing. Refrigerate leftovers.

Makes 12 servings.

SAUSAGE CRANBERRY-APPLE STUFFING

This is about 12 cups stuffing…enough for an 18-pound turkey.

2 pounds spicy turkey sausage or other bulk sausage

2 tablespoons corn oil
4 cups chopped red onion
4 cups chopped celery
2 tablespoons minced fresh garlic
2 tablespoons dried thyme
2 teaspoons dried sage leaves, crumbled
12 cups cubed bread (1-inch cubes), toasted
2 tart apples, diced
1 cup dried cranberries
1 cup dried apricots, chopped
½ cup chopped pitted prunes

2 cups chicken broth
salt and ground black pepper to taste

Crumble sausage in a skillet; stir and cook until browned; drain and place into a large bowl. Add corn oil, onions, celery, garlic, thyme and sage to skillet. Stir and cook over medium-low heat 15 minutes. Add to sausage in bowl. Add bread, apples, cranberries, apricots and prunes to bowl; toss.

Moisten mixture with chicken broth. Season with salt and pepper to taste. Use immediately or refrigerate.

Makes 10 servings.

WILD RICE APPLE-CRANBERRY STUFFING

Use real wild rice for a unique nutty flavor.

4 cups water
1 cup wild rice
1½ teaspoons salt, divided

½ cup butter
2 cups diced onion
2 cups diced celery
2 cups diced tart apples
¼ cup chopped fresh flat
   leaf parsley

1½ teaspoons dried sage leaf,
   crumbled
¼ teaspoon dried thyme, crushed
½ teaspoon ground black pepper
1 teaspoon salt
6 cups ½-inch-cubed crusty
   white bread, dried in oven
1 cup dried cranberries

1 cup chicken broth
2 tablespoons melted butter

Bring water to a boil in a heavy 2-quart saucepan. Add rice and salt.
Reduce heat to low; cover and cook until rice is tender and grains are split
open, about 1¼ hours (not all water will be absorbed). Drain and spread
rice out on a baking sheet to cool completely; set aside.

Melt butter in a large nonstick skillet over medium heat. Add onions and
celery; stir and cook 8 minutes. Add apples; stir and cook 5 minutes. Stir in
parsley, sage, thyme, pepper and salt; stir and cook 2 minutes. Mix in a
large bowl with cooled rice, bread cubes and cranberries.

Preheat oven to 450°.
Spoon stuffing into a buttered 13x9x2-inch baking dish. Drizzle with broth
and melted butter. Cover tightly with foil. Bake 20 minutes. Remove foil
and continue baking until top is lightly browned, about 15 minutes.
Refrigerate leftovers.

Makes 8 servings.

APPLE-CRANBERRY-SWEET POTATO BAKE

Substitute canned sweet potatoes, drained, if desired.

6 medium sweet potatoes peeled, cut into bite-sized pieces
¼ teaspoon salt

1 21-ounce can apple pie filling

1 8-ounce can whole cranberry sauce
2 tablespoons apricot preserves
2 tablespoons orange marmalade
¼ teaspoon ground cinnamon

Cover sweet potatoes with boiling water in a large saucepan; stir in salt.
Cook until tender, about 15 minutes; drain.

Preheat oven to 350°.
Spread apple pie filling into an 8x8x2-inch baking dish. Top evenly with
drained sweet potatoes.

Mix remaining ingredients in a small bowl; spoon over sweet potatoes.
Bake uncovered for 20–25 minutes or until thoroughly heated.
Refrigerate leftovers.

Makes 6 servings.

CRANBERRY-APPLE COMPOTE

A tasty side.

1 cup orange juice
1 teaspoon grated orange rind
1 3-inch cinnamon stick
4 cups fresh or frozen cranberries
1¼ cups diced peeled Granny Smith apple
½ cup maple syrup

In a large saucepan, mix orange juice, rind and cinnamon stick; bring to a boil and cook until reduced to ½ cup, about 5 minutes. Add cranberries and apples; cook over medium heat 10 minutes, stirring occasionally. Stir in syrup; cook 5 minutes. Discard cinnamon stick. Serve at room temperature. Refrigerate leftovers.

Makes 8 servings.

BRAISED RED CABBAGE
WITH CRANBERRIES

Use food processor to shred cabbage.

1 teaspoon corn oil
1 tablespoon brown sugar
3 large cloves fresh garlic, crushed
1 cup fresh cranberries, divided

5 cups shredded red cabbage
⅓ cup cranberry juice
3 tablespoons red wine vinegar
salt and ground black pepper to taste

In a large saucepan, cook and stir corn oil, sugar and garlic over medium heat 2 minutes. Stir in ½ cup cranberries. Cover and cook until cranberries pop, about 5 minutes.

Add cabbage, cranberry juice and vinegar. Cover and cook on low heat until cabbage is tender, about 20 minutes, stirring occasionally. Remove from heat; stir in remaining cranberries, salt and pepper to taste. Cover and let stand until cranberries are warm. Refrigerate leftovers.

Makes 4 servings.

CRANBERRY ACORN SQUASH

Serve warm...a nice side for baked ham.

1 cup fresh cranberries, chopped
1 cup coarsely chopped apple, unpeeled
½ teaspoon freshly grated orange peel
½ cup brown sugar, packed
pinch salt
2 tablespoons margarine, melted

4 small fresh acorn squash

Preheat oven to 350°.
Mix first six ingredients; set aside.

Cut squash lengthwise; discard seeds. Place squash cut-side down in a 13x9x2-inch baking pan. Bake 35 minutes. Turn squash cut-side up. Fill each with cranberry mixture, and continue baking about 25 minutes or until squash is tender. Refrigerate leftovers.

Makes 8 servings.

CRANBERRY RISOTTO

For best texture, serve immediately.

2 tablespoons butter or margarine
4 cloves fresh garlic, roasted
1 small onion, diced
¾ cup Arborio rice
2 cups chicken broth
¾ cup sweetened dried cranberries
1 tablespoon Parmesan cheese

Preheat oven to 425°.
Melt butter in a large saucepan. Add garlic and onion. Stir and cook over medium heat until soft. Add rice; stir and cook 2 minutes. Stir in broth and cranberries. Pour mixture into a greased casserole dish. Cover and bake 30 minutes. Stir in cheese. Refrigerate leftovers.

Makes 4 servings.

POMEGRANATE-CRANBERRY RICE PILAF

Serve with chicken and other meats.

1 fresh pomegranate

1 6-ounce package rice pilaf mix
½ cup sliced green onions
½ cup dried cranberries
¼ cup pine nuts, toasted
2 tablespoons shredded Parmesan cheese

Remove arils and seeds from pomegranate, set aside; discard peel and membrane.

In a medium saucepan, prepare rice mix according to package directions. Stir in reserved pomegranate arils and seeds, green onions, cranberries, pine nuts and cheese during the last 5 minutes of cooking. Serve warm.

Makes 4 servings.

SWEET POTATO CRANBERRY BAKE

A festive side dish.

2 15-ounce cans sweet potatoes, drained
1 8-ounce can crushed pineapple in juice, drained
2 tablespoons butter, melted
¼ teaspoon salt
⅛ teaspoon each—ground cinnamon, ground nutmeg
pinch of ground black pepper
1 large egg
1 16-ounce can whole berry cranberry sauce, divided

Preheat oven to 350°.
Mash sweet potatoes and pineapple. Stir in remaining ingredients except
½ cup cranberry sauce. Pour mixture into a greased 1½-quart casserole
dish. Top evenly with ½ cup reserved sauce. Bake 40 minutes.
Refrigerate leftovers.

Makes 8 servings.

SWEET POTATO CRANBERRY
CREAM CHEESE CASSEROLE

Cranberries add a tang to this delicious dish.

1 8-ounce can pineapple chunks, drained, reserve syrup
½ cup fresh orange juice
1 8-ounce package cream cheese, cubed
⅛ teaspoon ground nutmeg
pinch salt
2 17-ounce cans sweet potatoes, drained and sliced
½ cup sweetened dried cranberries
½ cup chopped pecans, divided

Preheat oven to 350°.
Add enough water to reserved syrup to measure ½ cup; place in a saucepan.
Add orange juice, cream cheese, nutmeg and salt. Stir over low heat until
smooth. Add sweet potatoes, cranberries and ¼ cup pecans; mix lightly.
Spoon mixture into a1½-quart baking casserole. Sprinkle with remaining ¼
cup pecans. Bake about 20 minutes or until hot. Refrigerate leftovers.

Makes 6 servings.

Beverages

CHAMPAGNE CRANBERRY PUNCH

Make a colorful ice ring with sweetened dried cranberries.

2 cups cranberry juice cocktail
1 12-ounce can frozen orange juice concentrate, thawed
1 cup fresh lemon juice
1 cup granulated sugar
1 375-milliliter bottle dessert wine
2 750-milliliter bottles champagne, chilled
ice ring

In a glass bowl, mix first four ingredients; chill 8 hours.

Pour chilled mixture into a chilled punch bowl. Stir in dessert wine and champagne just before serving. Add ice ring.

Makes 20 servings.

CITRUS CRANBERRY PUNCH

Pineapple, orange and cranberry juice…a very good punch.

1½ quarts cranberry juice cocktail, chilled
1 quart pineapple juice, chilled
1 quart orange juice, chilled
2 liters ginger ale, chilled
2 starfruit, cut into ¼-inch slices
fresh strawberries, halved
ice ring made with dried cranberries

In a large punch bowl, combine juices and ginger ale. Stir in starfruit and strawberries. Add ice ring. Serve chilled. Refrigerate leftovers.

Makes 20 servings.

CRANBERRY PUNCH WITH CRANBERRY ICE RING

Good punch for a holiday party.

2 cups crushed ice
1 cup fresh or frozen whole cranberries
4 ¼-inch fresh orange slices
3 32-ounce bottles cranberry juice cocktail, chilled, divided
2 25-ounce bottles non-alcoholic sparkling white grape juice, chilled

Place crushed ice in a 6-cup ring mold. Arrange cranberries and orange slices over ice. Pour 2 cups cranberry juice over fruit. Freeze ring at least 8 hours or overnight.

To serve, dip mold into warm water for 15 seconds. Carefully remove ring, and place, fruit side up, in a punch bowl. Add remaining cranberry and grape juice. Refrigerate leftovers.

Makes 24 servings.

WHITE CRANBERRY-LIME PUNCH

A refreshing punch.

1 64-ounce bottle white cranberry juice drink, chilled
1 ounce sweetened lime juice
1 pint lime sherbet, softened
6 ounces lemon-lime soda

Pour cranberry juice and lime juice into a large punch bowl. Scoop balls of lime sherbet into bowl. Stir in lemon-lime soda. Store in refrigerator.

Makes 12 servings.

GINGER CRANBERRY TEA

Garnish each serving with a cinnamon stick when serving.

3¼ cups cold water
¼ cup minced crystallized ginger
2 cups cranberry-raspberry blend juice
3 tablespoons granulated sugar
5 cranberry flavor herbal tea bags

Bring water and ginger to a boil in a large saucepan. Reduce heat. Add cranberry juice; simmer 5 minutes, stirring occasionally. Add sugar and tea bags; remove from heat and let stand 5 minutes. Discard tea bags. Serve warm.

Makes 5 cups.

HOLIDAY CRANBERRY TEA

Serve warm…add brewed orange herb tea to mixture as desired.

1 48-ounce bottle cranberry juice cocktail
1 cup brown sugar, packed
1 cup fresh orange juice
1 cup lemonade
1 cup pineapple juice
3 3-inch cinnamon sticks

Mix all ingredients in a large saucepan over low heat. Cook, until sugar is completely dissolved, stirring occasionally, about 10 minutes. Remove cinnamon sticks; serve warm.

Makes 8 servings.

CHERRY-CRANBERRY SHAKE

A frothy pink treat.

1 cup cranberry juice, chilled
1 cup cherry soda, chilled
1 tablespoon light cream
¾ teaspoon pure vanilla extract
1 cup vanilla ice cream

Process all ingredients in a blender until smooth. Serve immediately.

Makes 3½ cups.

CRANBERRY LEMONADE

Better make more than one serving…it's refreshing.

8 ounces cranberry juice blend
4 ounces lemonade

Mix in a large glass filled with ice. Garnish with lemon slice.

Makes 1 serving.

CRANBERRY SPRITZER

A refreshing treat…garnish with a lime wedge.

1 quart cranberry juice, chilled
½ cup fresh lemon juice, chilled
1 quart carbonated water, chilled
½ cup granulated sugar
1 cup raspberry sherbet, softened

Combine all ingredients; stir until blended. Serve immediately.

Makes 8 servings.

MULLED CRANBERRY DRINK

Garnish with whole cinnamon sticks when serving if desired.

1 48-ounce bottle cranberry juice drink
3 cups apple juice
3 cups orange juice
½ cup maple syrup
1½ teaspoons ground cinnamon
¾ teaspoon ground cloves
¾ teaspoon ground nutmeg

1 orange, sliced

In a large deep saucepan, bring all ingredients except orange to a boil. Add orange slices just before serving.

Makes 10 cups.

Sauces
Condiments

APRICOT-CRANBERRY SAUCE

A good sauce.

½ cup dried apricot halves, cut into ¼-inch strips
¾ cup cranberry juice cocktail
3 cups fresh cranberries
⅔ cup granulated sugar
1 tablespoon minced, peeled fresh ginger

Soak apricots in cranberry juice in a 2-quart saucepan for 10 minutes. Add remaining ingredients. Bring to a boil over high heat, then reduce heat to medium and cook uncovered until cranberries pop and mixture thickens a little, stirring occasionally, about 10 minutes. Spoon sauce into a glass serving bowl. Cover and refrigerate. Serve chilled.

Makes 2 cups.

CRANBERRY BBQ SAUCE

Baste ribs, chicken and other meats with sauce during the last minutes of grilling.

1 teaspoon corn oil
¼ cup chopped onion
1 cup whole berry cranberry sauce
½ cup maple syrup
¼ cup tomato ketchup
¼ cup cider vinegar

Heat corn oil in a medium saucepan over medium heat. Add onion; stir and cook until softened. Stir in remaining ingredients. Bring to a boil, then reduce heat and simmer uncovered 20 minutes, stirring occasionally. Process mixture in a blender until smooth. Spoon mixture into a glass jar. Store covered in refrigerator no longer than 1 week.

Makes 1 cup.

CRANBERRY DESSERT SAUCE

Serve over baked apples, ice cream and other good things.

1 16-ounce can whole berry cranberry sauce
½ cup caramel sauce
½ cup chopped pecans, toasted

Combine all ingredients in a saucepan over medium heat; stir until warm.
Spoon mixture into a glass bowl. Refrigerate leftovers.

Makes 2 cups.

CRANBERRY SWEET AND SOUR SAUCE

Dip your chicken nuggets in this tangy sauce.

¼ **cup brown sugar, packed**
1 **tablespoon cornstarch**

1 **cup whole berry cranberry sauce**
¾ **cup pineapple juice**
¼ **cup cider vinegar**
1½ **tablespoons soy sauce**

Stir brown sugar and cornstarch in a medium saucepan until blended. Stir in remaining ingredients. Cook over medium heat, stirring constantly, until mixture thickens. Spoon mixture into a glass container. Refrigerate.

Makes 2 cups.

ELSIE'S CRANBERRY SAUCE

Serve warm or chilled.

½ cup cranberry juice cocktail
½ cup cold water
½ cup granulated sugar
1½ cups fresh cranberries
¾ cup seedless red grapes
pinch ground ginger
pinch ground cloves

Bring juice, water and sugar to a boil in a medium saucepan, stirring until sugar is dissolved. Add remaining ingredients; bring to a boil. Reduce heat; cover and cook 15 minutes, stirring occasionally. Uncover and cook 10 minutes, stirring occasionally. Refrigerate leftovers.

Makes 6 servings.

JELLIED CRANBERRY SAUCE

Home-made sauce…tastes better!

1 cup granulated sugar
1 cup cold water
1 12-ounce package fresh or frozen whole cranberries

Mix sugar and water in a medium saucepan; bring to a boil. Add cranberries; return to a boil, reduce heat and simmer 10 minutes, stirring occasionally.

Place a wire mesh strainer over a bowl. Pour cranberry mixture into strainer. Press cranberries with the back of a metal spoon, until no pulp is left in the strainer, scraping the outside of strainer often.

Stir sauce. Pour into a glass container. Cover and cool completely at room temperature, then store in refrigerator.

Makes 1 cup.

WHOLE BERRY CRANBERRY SAUCE

Easy to prepare.

1 cup granulated sugar
1 cup cold water
1 12-ounce package fresh or frozen whole cranberries

Bring sugar and water to a boil in a medium saucepan. Add cranberries; return to a boil, then reduce heat and simmer 10 minutes, stirring occasionally. Cover and cool completely at room temperature. Spoon into a glass container. Refrigerate.

Makes 2 cups.

AVOCADO CRANBERRY SALSA

Serve with tortilla chips.

1 tablespoon fresh lime juice
2 tablespoons honey
1 minced jalapeño, seeds removed
¼ cup chopped red onion
2 ripe avocados, cut into ¼-inch pieces
¾ cup halved fresh cranberries
coarse salt and ground black pepper to taste

Whisk lime juice, honey, jalapeno and onion. Add avocados and cranberries. Season with salt and pepper; toss gently until mixed. Refrigerate leftovers.

Makes 4 servings.

CALIFORNIA CRANBERRY SALSA

Serve with chips and vegetables dippers.

¼ cup cranberry-raspberry juice blend

1½ cups diced fresh tomatoes
1 cup fresh cranberries, finely diced
1 medium-size ripe avocado, diced
½ cup fresh pineapple, diced
3 scallions, including tops, thinly sliced
2 tablespoons fresh lemon juice
1 jalapeño pepper, seeded and finely chopped
1 teaspoon crushed fresh garlic
pinch salt
fresh ground black pepper to taste

Bring cranberry juice to a boil in a small saucepan; boil until reduced to 1 tablespoon syrup, about 5 minutes; place in a medium serving bowl.

Add remaining ingredients; stir until blended. Chill. Refrigerate leftovers.

Makes 3 cups.

TEX-MEX CRANBERRY SALSA

Serve with nacho chips.

1 16-ounce can whole berry cranberry sauce
½ cup canned jalapeños, chopped
1 green onion, sliced
1 teaspoon dried cilantro
1 teaspoon ground cumin
1 teaspoon lime juice

Combine all ingredients in a glass bowl. Store leftovers in refrigerator.

Makes 2 cups.

CURRIED CRANBERRY-PEACH CHUTNEY

Delicious with ham and other meats.

1 cup cranberry-peach blend juice
½ cup chopped onion
½ cup chopped red pepper
2 teaspoons minced fresh garlic
1 6-ounce package sweetened dried cranberries

2 cans (15.25-ounce each) sliced peaches, drained and chopped
⅓ cup brown sugar, packed
1 tablespoon curry powder
1 tablespoon fresh ginger, minced
¼ teaspoon salt
⅛ teaspoon allspice

Combine first five ingredients in a medium saucepan. Bring to a boil over high heat, then reduce heat to medium. Add remaining ingredients; cook 15 minutes, stirring occasionally. Refrigerate up to 1 week or freeze.

Makes 4 cups.

EASY CRANBERRY CHUTNEY

Simple and tasty.

1 16-ounce can whole berry cranberry sauce
½ cup dark raisins
½ cup peeled and cored diced apple
6 tablespoons granulated sugar
6 tablespoons white vinegar
⅛ teaspoon ground allspice
⅛ teaspoon ground cinnamon
⅛ teaspoon ground ginger
pinch cloves

Mix all ingredients in a nonreactive saucepan. Cook over medium heat, stirring occasionally, until apples are tender and sauce is slightly thickened, about 30 minutes. Spoon mixture into a glass container. Store covered in refrigerator up to 1 week.

Makes 2 cups.

MANGO-CRANBERRY CHUTNEY

Serve at room temperature.

¼ cup olive oil
2 medium red onions, cut into ½-pieces
1 red bell pepper, diced
¼ cup peeled fresh ginger, minced
4 mangos, peeled and cut into ½-inch cubes
½ cup dried cranberries
1 cup unsweetened pineapple juice
½ cup cider vinegar
½ cup brown sugar, packed
1 tablespoon curry powder
1½ teaspoons dried hot pepper flakes
salt and ground black pepper to taste

Heat olive oil in a large heavy saucepan over medium-high heat. Add onions; stir and cook until softened. Add bell pepper and ginger; stir and cook 1 minute. Reduce heat. Add remaining ingredients; simmer, stirring occasionally until mixture thickens, about 15 minutes. Spoon mixture into a glass container. Store covered in refrigerator for up to one week.

Makes 7 cups.

NELAN'S CRANBERRY CHUTNEY

Serve with ham, turkey, pork or chicken.

1 cup chopped Granny Smith apple
1 cup raisins
1 cup chopped onion
1 cup granulated sugar
1 cup white vinegar
¾ cup chopped celery
¾ cup water
2 teaspoons ground cinnamon
1½ teaspoons ground ginger
¼ teaspoon ground cloves
1 12-ounce bag fresh or frozen cranberries

Bring all ingredients to a boil in a large saucepan. Reduce heat; simmer uncovered, stirring occasionally, until slightly thickened, about 30 minutes. Store in refrigerator up to 1 week.

Makes 4 cups.

CRANBERRY-PEAR CHUTNEY

Serve over roast turkey or ham.

¾ cup brown sugar, packed
½ cup dark raisins
½ cup white vinegar
1½ teaspoons finely chopped gingerroot
1 large clove fresh garlic, crushed
½ pound fresh cranberries
2 ripe firm medium size pears, chopped
¼ cup chopped onion
1 cup chopped red bell pepper

Mix all ingredients in a 2-quart saucepan; bring to a boil, stirring often, then reduce heat and simmer about 1 hour, stirring often, until mixture thickens and fruit is tender.

Spoon mixture into a glass container. Cover and refrigerate for no longer than 1 week.

Makes 2 cups.

CRANBERRY-MANGO RELISH

Great served with ham or turkey.

½ cup granulated sugar
½ cup brown sugar, packed
1 cup water
3 cups whole cranberries
1 cup diced fresh mango
1 tablespoon Dijon style mustard

In a medium saucepan, combine sugars and water. Bring to a boil over medium heat. Add cranberries. Bring to a boil, then reduce heat to low and simmer, stirring occasionally, until cranberries pop, about 10 minutes. Remove from heat; cool completely. Stir in mango and mustard. Cover and store in refrigerator.

Makes 6 servings.

CRANBERRY AND PICKLED BEET RELISH

Serve chilled or at room temperature, with poultry, beef or game.

½ **cup red wine vinegar**
½ **cup cold water**
⅔ **cup granulated sugar**
3 cups fresh cranberries
1 16-ounce jar sliced pickled beets, drained and quartered

Bring vinegar, water and sugar to a boil in a heavy 2-quart saucepan, stirring until sugar is dissolved. Add cranberries; bring to a boil, then reduce heat and simmer uncovered, stirring occasionally until cranberries pop and mixture is thick, about 20 minutes. Stir in beets. Remove from heat; cool. Store in refrigerator.

Makes 3 cups.

CRANBERRY RELISH

A good relish to make ahead...will keep at least 2 weeks.

1 16-ounce bag fresh cranberries
2 cups granulated sugar
½ cup cranberry juice
½ cup fresh orange juice
1 tablespoon grated orange zest

Combine all ingredients in a saucepan. Cook over medium heat until the cranberries pop, about 10 minutes. Skim foam. Cool to room temperature. Spoon into a sterilized glass container. Store covered in refrigerator.

Makes 10 servings.

MR. BROWN'S FRESH CRANBERRY RELISH

A favorite relish for that special turkey dinner.

4 cups fresh cranberries
2 large seedless navel oranges, do not peel, cut into 1-inch pieces
1 cup granulated sugar
½ cup Grand Marnier liqueur or cranberry juice

Cover and process cranberries and orange pieces, half at a time, in a large food processor bowl using the steel blade, pulsing on and off until finely chopped. Spoon mixture into a large glass bowl. Stir in sugar and liqueur or juice. Cover and chill well, overnight is best. Refrigerate leftovers.

Makes 10 servings.

PINEAPPLE-CRANBERRY RELISH

A delicious condiment.

**1 20-ounce can crushed pineapple in juice,
    drained, reserving juice**
water

2 12-ounce packages fresh cranberries
1¼ cups granulated sugar
1 cup chopped walnuts
1 tablespoon fresh lemon juice
¼ teaspoon ground cloves

Add enough water to reserved pineapple juice to measure 2 cups. Pour into a nonreactive saucepan.

Add cranberries and sugar. Stir over high heat until sugar dissolves and mixture comes to a boil. Continue to boil until cranberries pop and mixture is thick, stirring occasionally, about 10 minutes. Remove from heat. Stir in remaining ingredients. Spoon mixture into a glass bowl; refrigerate uncovered 2 hours before serving. Store covered in refrigerator.

Makes 6 cups.

CRANBERRY CATSUP

Good on those burgers and other meats.

1 tablespoon salad oil
3 tablespoons water
1 large onion, finely chopped

3 cups fresh cranberries
1 8-ounce can tomato sauce
1 cup granulated sugar
½ cup cider vinegar
½ teaspoon ground allspice

Place salad oil, water and onion in a 3-quart saucepan; cook and stir over medium-high heat until onion is tender.

Add remaining ingredients; bring to a boil over high heat, then reduce heat, and simmer uncovered until cranberries soften. Mash cranberries and stir mixture occasionally, until it is slightly thickened, about 20 minutes. Spoon catsup into a sterilized glass container. Cover and refrigerate for no longer than 1 week.

Makes 3 cups.

CRANBERRY SYRUP

Add a pinch of ground cinnamon for added flavor, if desired.

2½ cups cranberry juice
1 cup cranberries
¾ cup light corn syrup
¼ cup granulated sugar

Mix all ingredients in a medium saucepan; stir until sugar is dissolved. Bring mixture to a rolling boil over medium-high heat. Reduce heat to medium and boil 30–40 minutes or until mixture is reduced to 2½ cups. Pour syrup through a mesh strainer; discard cranberries. Store syrup covered in a glass container in refrigerator no longer than 1week.

Makes 2 cups.

CRANBERRY VINAIGRETTE

A good dressing for salad greens and fruit.

3 tablespoons olive oil, divided
2 tablespoons minced shallots or red onion

1 cup whole cranberries
½ cup cranberry juice
½ cup fresh orange juice

2 tablespoons red wine vinegar
2 tablespoons honey
¾ teaspoon salt
½ teaspoon freshly ground black pepper

Stir and cook shallots and 1 tablespoon olive oil in a small saucepan over medium heat until softened; set aside.

Bring cranberries, cranberry juice and orange juice to a boil in a small saucepan. Boil until reduced to 1 cup, about 10 minutes. Purée mixture in a blender with remaining olive oil, shallots, vinegar, honey, salt and black pepper until smooth. Pour vinaigrette into a glass container. Refrigerate.

Makes 1 cup.

Jams
Jellies
Marmalades
Conserves
Preserves

CRANBERRY-STRAWBERRY JAM

A special treat for breakfast toast.

1 quart fresh strawberries, chopped
2 cups fresh cranberries, chopped
4½ cups granulated sugar
3 tablespoons fresh lemon juice

half of a 6-ounce bottle of liquid pectin

Measure strawberries, adding enough water to make 2 cups. Mix all remaining ingredients except pectin in a large saucepan. Bring to a full rolling boil; boil hard 1 minute, stirring constantly. Remove from heat; stir in pectin at once. Skim off foam. Stir and skim 5 minutes. Ladle quickly into hot scalded sterilized jars leaving ¼-inch headspace. Seal as directed on purchased standard canning jar lids.

Makes 6 half-pints.

CRANBERRY JELLY

A pretty color and delicious flavor.

4 cups fresh cranberries
2 cups water
2 cups granulated sugar

In a large saucepan mix cranberries and water; cook over low heat until most of the cranberries have burst. Force through a coarse strainer. Return the purée to saucepan.

Add sugar and cook over low heat until sugar dissolves, swirling pan occasionally, then boil briskly, stirring frequently, to a jelly state (220° on candy thermometer) or until syrup drops in a sheet from a metal spoon and is as thick as desired when tested on a cold saucer. Immediately pour into hot sterilized pint jars. Seal immediately as directed on purchased standard canning jar lids.

Makes about 2 pints.

GRAPEFRUIT-CRANBERRY MARMALADE

Home-made marmalade…good.

4 medium grapefruit
1½ cups water
2½ cups fresh cranberries
3 cups granulated sugar

Using a vegetable peeler, remove rind from grapefruit; discard bitter white pith. Cut rind into julienne strips. Peel and section grapefruit; set aside.

In a large saucepan, mix rind, grapefruit sections and water; bring to a boil, then reduce heat to medium and simmer 15 minutes, stirring occasionally. Add cranberries; cook 10 minutes, stirring occasionally. Stir in sugar; cook 30 minutes or until slightly thickened, stirring occasionally. Pour in hot sterilized jars or airtight containers. Store in refrigerator no longer than 2 weeks.

Makes about 2 pints.

CRANBERRY CONSERVE

Serve this conserve chilled.

1 12-ounce bag fresh or frozen cranberries
1½ cups granulated sugar
1 cup water

1 tart apple, peeled, cored and chopped
zest of one orange, grated
juice of one orange
zest of one lemon, grated
juice of one lemon

½ cup raisins
½ cup currants
¾ cup chopped walnuts

In a saucepan, over low heat, cook cranberries, sugar and water until skins pop open. Add apple, zests and juices; cook 15 minutes. Remove from heat; stir in raisins and currants. Cool completely; stir in walnuts. Store in refrigerator for no more than 3 days.

Makes 4 cups.

CRANBERRY-RASPBERRY PRESERVES

Serve hot biscuits with cranberry-raspberry preserves.

6 cups fresh raspberries
2½ cups granulated sugar, divided
3 cups fresh cranberries
¼ cup fresh orange juice
grated zest of 1 orange

Stir raspberries and 1 cup sugar in a bowl; let stand 1 hour.

Stir cranberries and remaining sugar in a shallow nonreactive pan, and place over high heat, stirring constantly, until cranberries begin to release their juice, about 5 minutes. Continue cooking until cranberries pop and mixture is syrupy, and mixture comes to a boil. Skim foam that forms on top. Cook and stir until mixture thickens, about 10 minutes.

Add raspberries and all the juice that formed. Cook 10 minutes. Stir in orange juice and zest. Place a small amount of mixture on a saucer, and freeze 5 minutes. If mixture wrinkles when pushed to one side, it is done. If not, continue cooking 5 minutes and test again. Ladle into hot sterilized jars. Wipe rims clean with a clean damp towel. Seal with new lids and metal rings according to instructions on package. Process in a hot water bath 5 minutes. Remove from water bath. Check seals.

Makes 4 pints.

Miscellaneous

CRANBERRY GRANOLA

Home-made granola…a good way to start breakfast.

4 cups rolled oats
½ cup slivered almonds or chopped pecans
½ cup sweetened flaked coconut

1 teaspoon ground cinnamon
¼ teaspoon ground allspice
¼ teaspoon salt
½ cup cranberry-apple juice blend
¼ cup brown sugar, packed
¼ cup honey
2 tablespoons corn oil
1 cup sweetened dried cranberries
1 cup dry cereal (flakes or squares)

Preheat oven to 300°.
Mix oats, nuts and coconut in a bowl. In a medium saucepan, mix cinnamon, allspice, salt, cranberry juice, brown sugar, honey and corn oil. Bring to a boil. Pour over oat mixture; mix well.

Coat a baking sheet with nonstick cooking spray. Bake mixture until lightly browned, 30–40 minutes, stirring every 10 minutes. Stir in cranberries the last 10 minutes of baking. Remove from oven. Stir in dry cereal. Cool completely. Store airtight at room temperature up to 1 week.

Makes 16 servings.

CRANBERRY-RASPBERRY FONDUE

Serve dippers with wooden skewers or fondue forks.

1 tablespoon cornstarch
¼ cup water
1 16-ounce can jellied cranberry sauce
½ cup raspberry liqueur

Savory dippers
cocktail meatballs
chicken nuggets
cheese

Sweet dippers
cookies
coconut macaroons
pound cake

Combine cornstarch and water in a cup; set aside.

Whisk cranberry sauce in medium saucepan over medium heat until melted. Add liqueur; bring to a boil. Quickly stir in cornstarch mixture, stirring until mixture boils and is thickened. Pour mixture into a fondue pot; keep warm with low flame. Serve fondue with dippers of choice.

Makes 2 cups.

CRANBERRY TRASH MIX

Save some for yourself…the kids will like this!

1 16-ounce package candy corn
1 15-ounce package pretzel nibblers
1 12-ounce package caramel popcorn and peanuts
1 15-ounce package banana chips
1 15-ounce package candy-coated chocolate pieces, such as M&Ms
1 15-ounce package dried mango
1 15-ounce package dried pineapple
1 10-ounce package toffee pretzels
1 6-ounce package sweetened dried cranberries
1 6-ounce package worm-shaped chewy candy

Stir all ingredients in a large container. Store in an airtight container.

Makes 16 cups.

CRANBERRY TRUFFLES

Nice holiday treat.

2 cups fresh cranberries
¼ cup light corn syrup
¼ cup water

¾ cup butter
¾ cup unsweetened cocoa powder
1 14-ounce can sweetened condensed milk (not evaporated)

Toppings
chopped nuts
cocoa powder
powdered sugar
shredded coconut

In a medium saucepan, combine cranberries, corn syrup and water. Cook, stirring constantly, until cranberries pop and mixture is thickened. Remove from heat; cool completely.

Melt butter in a heavy saucepan over medium heat. Stir in cocoa, then stir in sweetened condensed milk. Stir mixture constantly until thickened. Stir in cooled cranberries. Refrigerate about 3 hours or until completely chilled. Shape into 1-inch balls.

Place each topping in a small dish. Roll balls in toppings. Place truffles in an airtight container and store in the refrigerator.

Makes 48 truffles.

About the Author

Theresa Millang is a popular and versatile cookbook author. She has written successful cookbooks on muffins, brownies, pies, cookies, cheesecake, casseroles and several on Cajun cooking. She has cooked on television, and contributed many recipes to food articles throughout the U.S.A.

Other Cookbooks by Theresa
The Best of Cajun-Creole Recipes
The Best of Chili Recipes
The Great Minnesota Hot Dish
The Joy of Blueberries
The Joy of Rhubarb

Notes

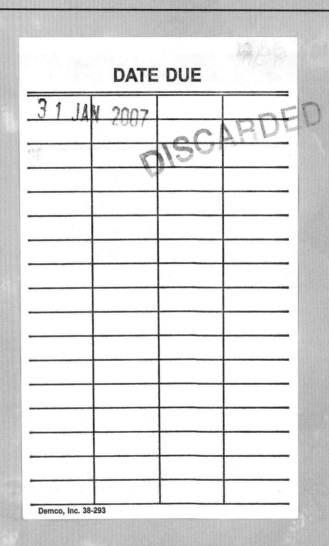